The First Finalists

The story of Rotherham United and the first ever League Cup Final

by

Adrian Booth

ISBN-10 1-903266-74-2
ISBN-13 978-1-903266-74-8

Barry Webster (left) was the first player ever to score a goal in a League Cup final. Roy Ironside (right) was the first goalkeeper ever to save a penalty in a League Cup final. The author (Adrian Booth, centre) met these two Millers heroes on 9th June 2005, and is honoured to be holding Barry's runners-up tankard. (Adrian Booth)

First published in 2007 by Irwell Press Ltd,
59A High Street, Clophill, Bedfordshire,
MK45 4BE.
Printed by Regal Litho, Milton Keynes

Contents

1. Introduction and Acknowledgements

Not even the most fanatical supporter of Rotherham United Football Club would claim that the Millers are numbered amongst the country's most successful teams. True, there has been the occasional triumph in the Sheffield County Cup, whilst the club famously reached Wembley on 14th April 1996, winning 2-1 against Shrewsbury Town in the final of the Auto Windscreens Shield (for teams in the bottom two divisions only). Other than that, United have twice made a foray to the 5th Round of the F.A. Cup (in 1952/53 and 1967/68), but even the club's secretary would be forced to admit it has never been necessary to strengthen the legs of the club's trophy cabinet! Only once have the Millers reached the final of a major national cup competition, and this was the inaugural Football League Cup in season 1960/61. Publication of this book early in 2007 marks forty six years since the Millers famously battled through to that final and, in the long intervening period, no Rotherham United side has ever come close to emulating that great feat. It was a wonderful campaign and this book outlines aspects of football in that era, provides details of the competition itself and Rotherham United's run to the final, and profiles the sixteen Millers players who were involved.

Being a football supporter aged in my mid-fifties, I can proudly say that I was numbered amongst the crowd of 12,226 that was present at that final (first leg), when second division Rotherham United took on first division Aston Villa at Millmoor on Tuesday 22nd August 1961. Although I was only eleven years of age at the time, I can nevertheless recall leaning on the front wall opposite the penalty spot (on the other side to where the players ran out on to the park) although all specific details of the game itself have now faded from my memory. The Rotherham United side on that great evening was: Roy Ironside, Peter Perry, Lol Morgan, Roy Lambert, Peter Madden, Ken Waterhouse, Barry Webster, Don Weston, Ken Houghton, Alan Kirkman and Keith Bambridge. During the earlier rounds George Darwin, Brian Jackson, Keith Kettleborough, Eddie O'Hara and Brian Sawyer also represented the club. Of these sixteen players, fourteen still live in northern England, one is in South Africa, and one is sadly deceased.

As that young lad, how could I possibly have imagined that, all these years later, I would speak personally to most of the players who created history in that great cup run? Whilst researching this book it has been my privilege to meet, in their homes, thirteen players who are now spread around northern England, with some visited two, three or even four times. These visits have been followed-up with various telephone calls, letters and e-mails. The players turned out to be thirteen very different characters but, what can be said about all of them, is that they were welcoming and friendly, and eager to help in any way they could. It has been a most enjoyable experience to talk to these fine 'old pros' about their careers in general and the cup run in particular, whilst enjoying tea and biscuits, having prized items from my own collection autographed, and being entrusted with the loan of treasured items of memorabilia. They are a great bunch and their individual career histories and memories are detailed later. Within the text, items enclosed in [square brackets] are additions to players' comments, added by the author.

I lived in Rotherham for thirty-five years, but can almost hear old friends and workmates saying: "How come Adrian Booth has written this book? He was a Sheffield United and Huddersfield Town supporter." Indeed I was, and perhaps a word of explanation is appropriate. I was born in July 1950 in the Pennine village of Thurlstone, but moved from there to Rotherham in 1953 when my dad (a Sheffield United supporter) got a job at the Swinden Laboratories of United Steel Companies on Moorgate. I was educated at Herringthorpe Junior School and Oakwood Secondary School. When I had developed an interest in football, my dad used to take me with him to watch the Blades. Meanwhile, we regularly had weekend visits to relations in Thurlstone and so my aunt (a lifelong Huddersfield Town supporter) used to take me to watch her team. The first League game I ever watched was Huddersfield Town versus Sheffield United at the old Leeds Road ground on Saturday 31st October 1959. However, I started going by myself to watch Rotherham United on 'spare' Saturdays. The first League game I attended at Millmoor was when Sheffield United visited on Saturday 8th April 1961, but I also regularly watched the Reserves play in the North Regional League, and got quite involved in the season when the championship was won, with goalkeeper Gordon Morritt playing part of the season as a centre forward and bagging over twenty goals! Over forty years later I was able to speak personally to Gordon about this and, on 1st June 2005, he told

The familiar Rotherham United programme cover which was used through the 1950s and into the 1960s. This is the author's programme from his first ever visit to Millmoor in April 1961, for the visit of local rivals Sheffield United. (Adrian Booth collection)

Reserves and I remember marking Colin Grainger, who gave me a real roasting for speed! So I told Danny perhaps it would be better if I tried centre forward, and that led to me scoring all those goals that season!" From the age of ten onwards, therefore, I regularly watched three clubs, and I now believe this instilled in me a more general football enthusiast ethic, rather than being a fanatical one-club man. All my school pals supported the Millers and my own affiliations led to friendly rivalries and much banter, especially when 'derby matches' took place. After I left school in July 1968 I worked for Rotherham Borough Council and a group of workmates regularly met for first team games at a specific spot on the Millmoor Lane side terrace. Meanwhile, I passed my driving test in late 1968 and was soon tripping off in my light blue C-registered Ford Anglia, making my own trips to Huddersfield Town, Rotherham United and Sheffield United matches, plus expanding my football watching to occasionally include Barnsley and Doncaster Rovers. In later years I quite often watched non-league Denaby United, but the one club I have steadfastly refused to watch is Sheffield Wednesday! Car ownership turned me into a 'ground hopper' and, at the time of writing, I have 'done' 87 of the 92 League grounds, achieved double figures of Scottish League grounds, and been to countless non-league matches.

It seems appropriate to share a few of my personal favourite memories of Rotherham United, while appreciating that all football fans are different and a game fondly remembered by myself may be nondescript to many others. I attended the match versus Stoke City on Saturday 16th December 1961, when near-pensioner Stanley Matthews attracted a crowd of 15,657, and I ran up Masborough Street in order to overtake hundreds of fans, all the while panicking that I was not going to get in. Stoke City won 2-1 with Stanley Matthews scoring the winner. Lol Morgan (who marked Matthews in that game) adds his own memories later. I was at Millmoor when S.C. Telstar visited on Monday 2nd May 1966 and won 2-0, the Dutch visitors then being the first foreign club I had ever seen. I was also there on 20th January 1974 when Rotherham United kicked off at 2pm versus Northampton Town in the first Sunday match ever played at Millmoor. To get round Sabbath laws of the era, admission was by purchasing a duplicated single sheet A5 size 'programme' which simply listed the teams. I became quite enthralled during the 1974/75 Fourth Division promotion campaign, and went on car trips with my work mates to

me: "At the time Danny Williams was manager and was deciding between Roy Ironside and myself for first team goalkeeper. I was having a spell in the Reserves when, one particular week, Danny informed me he wanted to give a trial to another goalkeeper. I told Danny that, if he was short of players, I would be happy to play centre half, just to get a game, so Danny picked me in that position. The game was away at Port Vale some away games. The journey to Crewe Alexandra on 5th March 1975 proved quite eventful, when four of us took the Wednesday afternoon off work and travelled by car in ever thickening fog. The driver on that awful journey was Paul Wickson, my then workmate who went on to become the Millers' long-standing action photographer and programme contributor. Fog ruined the match and we could not see one goalmouth, only realising Crewe Alexandra had scored when the players loomed out of the fog to take up their positions to re-start the game. Crewe Alexandra won the game 1-0. My favourite player in that fondly remembered side was Tommy Spencer, a giant of a centre back and a wonderful defensive organiser. I was at Millmoor on Saturday 1st January 2005 for the game versus Coventry City which just about condemned hero manager Ronnie Moore to the departure lounge and, strangely, was also Peter Reid's last game in charge of Coventry City. And to bring us up to date, I was at the Millers' ignominious home defeat to Colchester United on 12th November 2005.

Since March 1988 my wife Janet (a Denaby lass) and myself have lived in Bridlington. Expanding upon my general football watcher ethic, I have subsequently regularly attended Scarborough matches, plus York City and many local non-league clubs, although visits to my roots have kept me in touch with the Blades, Town and Millers. These days I am also a member of the Rotherham United Nostalgia Society and whenever possible, despite a 150 mile round trip, attend its highly recommended meetings. On a personal note, my mother, two married sisters, nieces and nephew, and several old friends still live in Rotherham.

It is my pleasure to thank all the people who have helped in various ways whilst I have been writing this book, namely: Keith Bambridge, Graham Barnes, Janet Booth, Barrie Dalby, Ken Houghton, Roy Ironside, Keith Kettleborough, Alan Kirkman, Roy Lambert, Mavis Lambert, Barry Lyons, Peter Madden, Johnny Meynell, Lol Morgan, Gordon Morritt, Peter Perry, Paul Rickett, Brian Sawyer, Frank Tweddle, Ken Waterhouse, Dorothy Waterhouse, Barry Webster and Don Weston. I would like to expand upon four of the credits: I only have three programmes from the cup run in my collection, and Graham Barnes kindly loaned me his own copies from the other matches in order that I could complete the illustrations for this book, plus loaned various photographs from his collection; Barrie Dalby answered several queries, provided research material, and gave me the home addresses of most Millers players who featured in the cup run, so enabling me to write to them to request interviews; Peter Perry kindly loaned me irreplaceable items from his personal collection, which are duly credited; while Keith Bambridge also loaned me personal items and (although neither he nor I realised it at the time) proved to be the catalyst for this book as a result of two lengthy chats at his home in Bramley. I have obtained information from *Millmoor Personalities 1946-86* by David Watson, *The Definitive Rotherham United* by Gerry Somerton, certain other books credited in the text, and various internet web sites. Thanks also to Rotherham Library (Local Studies Section) for supplying photocopies of 1960 and 1961 newspaper match reports, and to the *Rotherham Advertiser* and *Sheffield Star* newspapers for permission to reproduce them. I made a decision to

reproduce the reports verbatim, as they give a lovely 'feel' for the era under consideration, and dramatically display how radically the style of football reporting has changed over the last forty six years. It will become apparent when reading these old news reports that, in odd places, the sentences perhaps do not flow. The wording used herein is reproduced exactly as it originally appeared. During my researches I purchased photographs depicting Brian Sawyer, Andy Smailes and Ken Waterhouse, plus twelve Aston Villa players, from *Sporting Collectibles* of Leicester, and I thank proprietor John Fitzhugh for granting permission to reproduce them. I further thank Brian Sawyer, Roy Lambert and Barrie Dalby who kindly read my manuscript, since it was important to have the text checked by players who were actively involved at the time (Brian and Roy) and by a lifelong Rotherham United supporter (Barrie).

In conclusion, it will become apparent that George Darwin is the only accessible ex-Millers player without a detailed profile and current photograph, despite me spending eight months trying to find him. I can only state that I wrote four letters to football clubs and associations (none of whom deigned to reply), made certain other enquiries, and personally asked over twenty ex-Rotherham United players if they were aware of George's whereabouts. Unfortunately, at the time of writing, it has not proved possible to interview George, but Keith Bambridge has stepped into the breach by providing memories of Darwin's vital contribution to the away match at Leicester City, and in addition has given a nice tribute to a fine old fellow professional.

Adrian Booth, Bridlington.
November 2006

The author's treasured football autograph book contains a host of stars from the early 1960s. The two pages reproduced here bear the signatures of over thirty Rotherham United players, including Danny Williams, all the cup final squad, the sadly deceased Brian Jackson and Brian Tiler, plus then up-and-coming stars such as Barry Lyons, Ian Butler, Albert Bennett, Frank Casper and David Carver. (Adrian Booth)

2. Setting the Scene

The *Chambers Concise Dictionary* defines nostalgia as a 'sentimental longing for past times'. One should not long for the impossible, namely to go back to far off past times, but it is certainly a pleasant occupation to reminisce with affection. When Rotherham United FC embarked on its inaugural Football League Cup campaign in season 1960/61, practically every aspect of the game was different to how it is now, and so initially we shall take a nostalgic look back at how things used to be. Not to claim that the game then was better or worse, for every individual supporter will have his own opinion as to which was football's golden era. But simply to look at the game and its infrastructure around 1960, after a century of evolution; a scenario which was simply accepted as 'the norm' by that era's supporters, even if there were seeds of unrest amongst the players. Thinking back 46 years, the game then seemed to be watched more for its own sake in a generally no-nonsense fashion, whilst the general lifestyles, attitudes and culture of people from that period seem quite remote from ours of today. Just about everything then seems so different from the high profile modern game – awash with money, hype and razzmatazz – and it is interesting, particularly for the benefit of supporters who were not around then, to look back to season 1960/61.

At that time the **League Structure** was the long standing traditional system, which is used throughout this book. Division One, as it was then, is now re-branded as the Premiership, whilst Division Two is now the Championship, Division Three is now Division One, and Division Four now Division Two. Back in season 1960/61, the top division included Cardiff City, Blackpool and Preston North End. Sheffield United were winning promotion out of Division Two, whilst the second tier also included Swansea Town (they were not called City then), Scunthorpe United and Lincoln City. Crystal Palace were a Fourth Division team. Other clubs which were then members of the Football League were Accrington Stanley, Aldershot, Barrow, Bradford Park Avenue, Newport County, Southport and Workington.

A 1960/61 team group of Rotherham United, showing twelve players, of whom eleven represented the club in the cup run. Back row, left to right are: Ken Houghton, Colin Smith, Brian Sawyer, Roy Ironside, Ken Waterhouse and Peter Madden. Front row, left to right are: Barry Webster, Lol Morgan, Keith Kettleborough, Alan Kirkman, Roy Lambert and Peter Perry. The 'odd man out' (Colin Smith) was a centre forward signed from Hull City in June 1960. He only played that season and scored 3 goals in his 9 appearances. (Adrian Booth collection)

The **stadiums** at which League matches were played were generally fairly basic. The average ground would have terracing on four sides, often with a grandstand on one side only, and probably then with a section of terracing in front of it. The seats in the grandstand were normally wooden. Toilet facilities were quite primitive. Much of the terracing was uncovered and supporters had to brave whatever weather was thrown at them during a game. **Crowd control** was purely the preserve of the local Police, and it was quite common to have a five-figure crowd with just a few policemen on duty. But crowds then were well behaved and opposing supporters mingled freely, leading to enjoyable exchanges of banter. Marauding gangs of bare-chested chanting thugs were unheard of. It was to be many years, and prompted by the Hillsborough and Bradford City disasters, before stadiums were modernised, with widespread all-seater facilities, and the introduction of Ground Safety Certificates and teams of safety stewards. An average match **programme** was generally about a dozen pages, and usually comprised a few club notes, visiting player details, team line-ups and fixtures, and was in black and white throughout with few, if any, photographs. The price was usually 3d, which roughly equates to one new penny! Rotherham United's programme in 1960/61 featured the same basic front cover design which had been used from the early 1950s, with the red high kicking footballer in action. Compare this with modern eighty page, glossy, profusely illustrated, expensive, match day magazines, the covers of which are covered in sponsors' logos.

Other **publicity** for football was mostly in the form of gossip and match reports in local newspapers, plus a small number of national magazines (for example *Soccer Star* and *Charles Buchan's Football Monthly*), with the days of the Internet, Ceefax, videos, Match of the Day, live matches on television, pundits, and DVDs being light years away. Browsing through one of those contemporary football magazines is now an exercise in pure nostalgia. The *Football Monthly* magazine (founded in 1951) for example cost 1s 6d per issue and was filled with articles by players, news items, letters, transfer dealings, and photographs. Advertisements for balls, stockings and boots were prevalent, whilst the RAF were seeking recruits at £8 10s 0d a week. But it is some of the 'small ads' for memorabilia that are quite fascinating. For example you could be the proud owner of an automatic pen with the name of your club engraved on it by sending a postal order for 2s 6d (plus 3d for postage). There were 113 teams to chose from including Barrow, Rotherham United, Workington, and even Third Lanark, with the company claiming: "Press and the writing point appears. Press again ... and, hey presto! it has gone." In 1961, that was real state of the art goods. The Collectors Club offered postcard size photographs of players at one shilling each or ten for seven shillings, and that included postage and packing. Sadly no Rotherham United players were included amongst the list of available players. From one advertiser you could buy a rosette of any club for 1s 3d, whilst another sold embroidered stick-on cloth badges of 48 different clubs (including the Millers) at 2s 4d including postage. [*author's note*: I have still got a Sheffield United embroidered badge in my collection to this day!] Many programme dealers sold brand new stock from 3d each, or you could get 'assorted bundles' by sending a postal order for either 2s, 5s, 10s – not forgetting to add 4d to cover postage. Those were the days!

Out on **the pitch** it was all very different in that era. Hard wearing modern turf, groundsmanship, and under-soil heating, had not been invented. By the time winter was well set in, the grass on an average pitch had worn away, and games were played on bare earth apart from triangles of grass near each corner flag. Some pitches could degenerate into a sea of mud during periods of rain and snow. The **match ball** was not the modern lightweight plastic type, inflated with a pump. When playing on a wet or muddy pitch, the leather ball became impregnated with water and was very heavy to head, and difficult to kick over long distances. For example, a goalkeeper taking a drop kick from the edge of his penalty area might only just land the ball on the centre line. Speaking on 10th June 2005, the great Rotherham United stalwart Roy Lambert recalled: "In those days you could have a laugh with the referee. I remember one match when the ball became really heavy in rain and mud. As the referee was jogging past me I joked – you'll need to allow the goalie two kicks to get the ball out of his area!" The **referee** wore a very angular black jacket, and any player bookings were simply written into his notebook. There were no yellow cards to brandish. A sending-off was indicated by a booking and a raised arm pointing to the tunnel, with no red cards in use. Out on the touch-lines, assistance was given by two linesmen (not Referee's Assistants) of which one carried a red flag and one a yellow. **Players' positions** in that era were referred to as full backs, half backs, centre half, wingers, inside forwards, and centre forward. It was then universal in match programmes to show the players lined up in 1-2-3-5 formation, as follows:

Outside Left   Centre Forward   Outside Right

Inside Left   Inside Right

Left Half   Centre Half   Right Half

Left Back   Right Back

Goalkeeper

which sheds moisture. In those days the ball was made up of a series of stitched leather panels with a lace tie-up and was Squad numbers had not then been thought of and, out on the pitch, there was no such thing as player number 28 tackling the opponents' number 37. In 1960/61 the goalkeeper was number 1 (although he rarely carried the number on his back), the right back wore number 2, the left back 3, right half 4, centre half 5, left half 6, outside right 7, inside right 8, centre forward 9, inside left 10 and outside left 11. This was universal in every team. There were also **no substitutes** allowed and, if a player was injured, he would try his best to stay on the pitch, if only to be of 'nuisance value' and possibly be put out on the wing. Peter Perry recalls one match when he was badly fouled in the first half when his opponent's studs gashed his flesh just above the ankle. During the half time interval he pulled down his bloodstained sock, the doctor cleaned the wound and put four stitches in, and he was told "get back out". He still has the scar to this day. If a player was so badly injured that he had to leave the field of play, the team carried on with ten men. When a player missed a game through injury, he literally lost his shirt to the replacement. **Players' kit** was quite plain and basic at all clubs, with the same style retained year after year. There were no replica kits on sale, no changing the shirt design every season, and none of the modern style embellishments such as logos and sponsor's names on the chest. Rotherham United's kit in season 1960/61 was a plain red shirt with quite a deep v-neck, short sleeves with a thin white trim, plain white shorts, and white socks with a red roll-over top. The shirt did not even carry the club's crest, and had just a white number on the back. As regards shorts, they were only just becoming accepted under that terminology, having long been known as 'knickers'. Goalkeepers were officially allowed to wear a choice of stipulated colours of jersey, although the majority chose plain green. The jerseys were often wool, with a roll neck. Co-ordinated full kits were not allowed, and the goalkeeper's shorts and socks had to match those of the outfield players. The players' **boots** were also very different to those worn by modern day players. In the early 1960s more lightweight boots, with moulded soles and rubber studs, were just coming into widespread use. Players such as Jimmy Greaves (Zephyr), Danny Blanchflower (Simlam 'Italia' at 58s 6d) and Bobby Charlton (Bozeat 'Champion' at 57s 11d) put their names to such modern footwear. Speaking on 26th July 2005, Keith Bambridge related some interesting tales regarding slightly earlier footwear: "The boots we wore in the 1950s were leather, fitted quite high round the ankle to give support and protection, and had a reinforced toe cap. The studs were nailed into the soles. When we got to the ground, all the players used to go out with the trainer to assess how hard the pitch was, and this determined the length of studs to be worn, depending on if the pitch was hard or muddy. Albert Wilson and Mark Hooper were the trainers in those days, and part of their standard equipment at all games was a steel hobbing foot [a last]. When we got in from the pitch inspection, the trainers then worked hard on preparing all the players' boots, adjusting stud lengths, which involved taking the hard top off (if we needed short studs for the game) or nailing extra leather on if we needed longer studs. This procedure was, of course, wide open to problems. If there was a dramatic change in weather between the 2pm pitch inspection and the game, there could be some frantic activity altering studs. I remember one winter's game at home to Darlington when half the pitch was icebound in the shadow of the stand, whereas the other half was soggy where the sun had got to it. When we swapped sides of the pitch after half time, all the players' studs became unsuitable! Another problem was that, if the pitch was rock hard, the nails could begin to work through the bottom of your boots (which gave you blisters) or come right through and puncture the skin on the soles of your feet. After I had played my second match for United at home to Notts County [17th September 1955, draw 1-1] the ball of my foot turned septic and I had to report to Millmoor on the Sunday for medical treatment. The club doctor took out his scalpel and lanced the affected part of my foot, and some puss shot out. We heard a loud bang behind us and turned to see that a fellow player had fainted! Boots then were relatively supple but, when brand new, were not suitable for match use. On each occasion when I had a new pair of boots, trainer Mark Hooper, who was of similar stature and shoe size, used to take it upon himself to wear them for a few days at training until they were 'broken-in', so protecting my feet, and I could then wear them at the next match."

Another thing that impacted on the game, although perhaps not immediately appearing relevant, was **National Service** and, later in the book, the players refer to their own experiences. At the end of World War 2 the government had armed forces desperate to return to home life, but it was committed to enforcing the terms of surrender on Germany and Japan, plus having occupation and security duties around the world. The need for men was greater than normal voluntary recruitment and the upshot was the establishment of National Service, under the terms of an Act of Parliament which came into force at the beginning of 1949 and ran to the last intake of men in 1960. Under the terms of the Act, it was compulsory for able-bodied young men to serve two years in the armed forces and Rotherham United footballers, who fitted neatly into this category and era, were all forced to leave Millmoor and do their stint. In fact altogether 1.13 million men were conscripted, the majority serving in the Army. It was a time of great camaraderie, with young men from different backgrounds thrown together in a strange situation. But they learned new skills, and many visited foreign countries at a time when world travel was a rarity – although some had to face combat situations and lost their lives. Each conscript (and that includes the Rotherham United players) faced initial registration, assessment and a medical examination, an interview to match him to a suitable unit, eight to twelve weeks basic training, a regulation haircut, early rising, shouting sergeants, drill, other training, army food, communal sleeping and washing in barracks, the requirement to look after kit, and harsh military discipline with punishment for misdemeanours. Entertainment was generally in the NAAFI, whilst conscripts were entitled to fourteen days leave after eight months, plus weekend leave. On occasions this enabled certain professional players to fit-in a game of football, but basically National Service cost most professionals two years out of their careers. The Army did encourage all sports, as playing games kept servicemen fit, and inspired teamwork and leadership skills. For some of the very best sportsmen, the ability to play well led to an easier life, being excused military duties to allow time for training and playing in matches. The very best played in high profile representative games, and this was an experience enjoyed by several Rotherham United players.

In 1960/61 the **average match** was probably played at a slower pace than that of today, and was more structured than the fast and fluid modern game. Players then tended to stick more to their allocated position on the pitch and, for example, United's outside right Barry Webster recalls being told by the manager: "Hug the right wing touchline. If you just put in six good crosses during a match you have done your job." Everybody knew what position any individual was playing by the number on his back: for example the number 2 right full back would always mark the opposition's number 11 outside left, number 3 would mark 7, and 5 mark 9. When the match was about to kick off, the teams lined up in 1-2-3-5 formation (shown above) but, as soon as the game got underway, they did not actually play in that formation, but adopted what were later more formally classified as 'modern' 4-2-4 or 4-4-2 formations. Games tended to be played more to an accepted structure with, as a general rule, players taking the field without any detailed pre-planned tactics, or a 'game plan' to use modern parlance. Furthermore, back in 1960/61, it was normal for the eleven players to run out on to the pitch a mere five minutes before kick off. Compare this to the build-up to a 'modern' game where the sixteen man squad and several coaches are all out on the pitch three quarters of an hour before kick off undertaking numerous jogging and exercising routines in order to warm-up players' muscles and so avoid unnecessary pulls and strains once the match proper gets underway.

It is surely not just nostalgia, for the players' whole **attitude** to playing is recalled as being different back in 1960/61. Football then was played in an era when players endeavoured to stay on their feet during a match and it was almost a point of honour not to go down after a bad tackle. The game was played tough and hard but players did not fake injuries, whilst attempts at blatant cheating were practically unheard of. The 1960/61 Millers forwards would have stoically endured numerous over-robust tackles, but can you imagine any one of them hurling himself pole-axed on to the turf, writhing and clutching at his shin, with face contorted in agony (as is second nature to many modern professionals), trying to get a fellow player booked – and all this at the merest brush of an opponent's leg? Can you recall them blatantly diving, when lightly touched by a defender's little finger, to cheat the referee into awarding a penalty? If a player crashed to the ground in those days, the chances were high that it was a genuine foul or penalty. As regards personal discipline, the players generally deferred to the referee's authority, even when the official gave a dodgy decision. The modern 'norm' of rushing up to a referee after a decision goes against your side, to jostle the official, whilst snarling, scowling, strutting and raging simply did not happen back then. Watch any top level game in 2006/07 and you will almost certainly see cheating, blatant diving, reckless physical assaults and referee bating, with a possibility of spitting, head-butting, elbowing and general bad attitude. The post match interviews will include mandatory whingeing about incompetent officials. This is not to say that the 1960/61 players were whiter than white; it was a tough man's game and things did go on, but not to the excesses of today.

What actually happened in 1960/61 in the **build up** to a game? During a fascinating chat about these matters on 23rd May 2005, Roy Lambert recalled: "In all my time at

Millmoor in the 1950s I cannot recall once, ever, working out tactics and a game plan before a match. During the week, the manager was a 'suit' who would be doing administration work, and it was the trainers who got involved with the players, keeping us fit. Preparations for the next match were basically left to the players and we used to dictate things ourselves. On occasions we might go and spy on another team, but this was at the discretion of the players and was done off our own bat. For example, if we were due to play, say Sunderland away in a fortnight, and they were playing a mid-week game at Sheffield United, perhaps Peter Madden and myself would go along and watch. We would then pass on tit-bits we picked up, such as any good players they had who needed watching, or perhaps we might have noticed that their goalkeeper was weak on crosses, etc. If the Saturday match was at Millmoor, the players would all arrive by 2pm and the manager would be in charge, having selected the side to play. It was then a case of every player preparing for the game in his own personal way. Some would get changed into their kit immediately and then just sit quietly, mentally preparing themselves for the game. Some liked to smoke a cigarette. Some liked to lie on the bench and have liniment rubbed into their legs by the trainer, whilst others did stretching exercises such as touching toes and star jumps. Goalkeeper Roy Ironside always used to go into the shower area and repeatedly bounce a ball back off the wall to warm up his reflexes. I personally only got changed about quarter of an hour before kick off. When we went out onto the pitch we usually had two balls with us, one for the defence and one for the forwards, and we would just kick them around while the two captains were tossing up with the referee. As we lined up before kick off we always used to stand in the 1-2-3-5 formation, but this was more for the benefit of the crowd, just to show who was playing in each position. We certainly did not play like that when the game started. Taking the 1960/61 side for example, centre half Peter Madden would immediately drop back to play between the two full backs, Lol Morgan and Peter Perry, who would pivot either side of him. If we were defending, those three would be supported by a defensive wing half, usually myself, which effectively created a back four. The other half back, Ken Waterhouse, who was a very creative player, would be in mid-field together with one of the inside forwards who would drop back, and the two wingers would also drop back. Thus the actual defensive playing system equated to what became known as 4-4-2. If we were attacking, the wingers would be expected to keep wide, up in the opponents' half, and so the actual formation then became 4-2-4. There was a bit of freedom within the system. For example if we were attacking down the left wing, left-half Ken Waterhouse would go forward while I (as right-half) would undertake defensive cover, whereas if we attacked down the right, Ken would cover back for me. Our attacks could also involve the full backs, with Lol Morgan and Peter Perry pivoting forward round Peter Madden, depending on which side of the field the ball was, with one covering for the other. We actually used to play 4-2-4 and 4-4-2 long before modern coaches 'invented' and put a name to such systems. In those days it was unheard of for a manager to be standing on the touchline, waving his arms and screaming instructions at the team. Senior players would look after youngsters and pass on tips and advice during play. If things were not going well out on the pitch a couple of senior players would have a quick chat and try to sort things out. The first manager we had at Millmoor who was not a 'suit' was Tom Johnston. He was a qualified F.A. coach and used to get involved in training, and he liked to try out new ideas." [see Chapter 9]

Back in 1960/61 it was not just the foregoing aspects that were different. The whole **make-up of teams** and how the game was administered was different. For example, most South Yorkshire football supporters who were around in the early 1960s and before will recall a side that represented their club in that era. Such fans will be able to name all the players, who probably stayed together for several seasons, and a regular eleven whose names roll off the tongue like the lyrics of a well loved pop song. The Rotherham United side that played in the 1960/61 season League Cup Final is a case in point, with their names listed in the second paragraph of the Introduction. In the 'old days', professional teams, as a general rule, comprised mostly of fairly local players. After all, the average journeyman footballer was probably installed in his home (possibly a club house) with his local wife, had the kids established at school, and was quite happy playing for his local professional club which he had supported from being a young boy. In addition, it was still the era of the football **maximum wage**, and why would a player uproot from Rotherham when the wage on offer at any other club would be exactly the same? When interviewed for this book, Rotherham United's long serving full back Lol Morgan mentioned that, when he signed for the Millers, he received a £10 signing-on fee and at one time they had a full team of local £10-ers with no outside signings. Obviously this was not a hard and fast rule – plenty of players

A Millers training session about 1960, against a backdrop of C.F. Booth Ltd's scrap yard, and providing a stark contrast with modern day purpose-built training centres. The playing surface is red shale. In the foreground are: Ernest Jackson (extreme left, in the white shirt, the club trainer and former Sheffield United player) who is playing the ball, Peter Perry (second left, wearing a pair of 'sneakers') moving in to tackle, a slim Ken Waterhouse (in the centre, in striped socks) with eyes on the ball, and Eric Robinson (extreme right) who is scratching his back. The three players in the background are: Barry Webster (extreme left, half turned away) with white patch on the shoulder, Brian Jackson (second left) standing with hands on hips, and Harold Hughes (centre) running behind Ken Waterhouse. Hughes played just a single game for the United first team (in September 1959) whilst Eric Robinson played thirteen games and scored one goal. Roy Lambert recalls: "That equipment in the scrap yard included a large steel ball which was raised and then dropped on to scrap to break it up. We often had to take cover as bits of scrap came flying over on to our training area. Also, there were often holes broken in the corrugated sheeting at the rear of the terracing!" The club's gymnasium, which was opened in 1966 at a cost of around £35,000, now stands on this site. (Peter Perry collection)

did move around the country – but generally speaking a high percentage of club squads would be from a reasonably local catchment area.

Players often clocked-up several hundred games for one team and clubs regularly kept more or less the same squad for several years. Older supporters in South Yorkshire will no doubt remember Sheffield United's legendary defence in the late 1950s/early 1960s that long comprised England International goalkeeper Alan Hodgkinson, full backs Cecil Coldwell (the captain) and Graham Shaw (another England international), and half backs Brian Richardson, Joe Shaw and Gerry Summers, who seemingly played together for year after year, and none ever got injured! This defence was coupled with a front five in the early 1960s that more often than not comprised Len Allchurch, Billy Russell, Derek 'Doc' Pace, Billy Hodgson and Ron Simpson.

This rule of thumb started to die out after the **abolition of the maximum wage**. Speaking about this on 14th May 2005, ex-Rotherham United forward Brian Sawyer commented: "Prior to the abolition of the maximum wage, then set at £20 per week, plus £4 for a win and £2 for a draw, any player's contract was for one year only. However, the club had the option to retain the player indefinitely. No player could move to another club unless his current club literally sold him. They could of course sack him at the end of the year by giving him a 'free'. Jimmy Hill, the elected leader of the Player's Union, [the PFA] started a campaign to change this iniquity.

We the players wanted a contract that was equal for both sides. We wanted a contract for a mutually agreed period of time, which left both parties free of their obligations at its end. Jimmy Hill obtained a unanimous mandate to strike for such a contract from meetings across the country. These meetings were full of representatives from every club and all the leading players of that time. We had the press witness and photograph our unanimity. Club directors, however, were equally fiercely opposed to this change. They offered instead the abolition of the maximum wage and in a brilliant propaganda move Tommy Trinder, then the Chairman of Fulham, publicly offered to pay Johnny Haynes £100 per week. Jimmy Hill called together further meetings across the country, with the one I attended in Manchester a paltry travesty of the previous meeting with all the leading players (with the honourable exception of England full back Tommy Banks of Bolton Wanderers) notable by their absence. We kept the press out and meekly accepted the no maximum wage option. Jimmy Hill likes to accept plaudits now, but as Tommy Banks said forcibly at the time, quite simply we were bought off. It was to be many more years following the George Eastham court case and finally the Bosman ruling before players obtained an equal contract."

The 'restraint of trade' rights won by George Eastham (he had wanted to move from Newcastle United to Arsenal but was prevented from doing so) plus the parallel growing popularity of private car ownership and the vast improvements to the national road network, made both commuting and moving between clubs more feasible. Especially from the 1970s onwards (and past the Millennium) there was wholesale mass movement of players between clubs, whose squads drastically altered in each and every close season. Mid-season transfers to freshen-up a squad became commonplace. The 'football mercenary' had arrived, with players moving to whichever club would pay them the highest wages. Each professional football club was, after all, simply a reflection of the area it represented, where once tight-knit communities had became fluid with children growing up to go and live and work in all parts of the country. Why should footballers be any different? In 1960/61 most clubs' players would be reasonably local white lads, with coloured players (such as Charlie Williams at Doncaster Rovers) quite a rarity. Compare this with any present day South Yorkshire side, which will have an ever-changing flow of players from all over the country, and of several ethnic backgrounds.

So many things are different when comparing football in 1960/61 with today, and the natural course of evolution means it could not be otherwise. If a group of supporters of different ages got together in the pub, all would lay claim to their favourite era's players being the best. But how can anybody really say if Peter Madden or Paul Stancliffe was the best ever Millers centre half, or if Roy Ironside was a better goalkeeper than Mike Pollitt? One matter needs to be addressed, however, and that is how Rotherham United's 1960/61 cup final side would fare in the modern game. These players were good enough, in their day, to play in the Second Division of the Football League and get their club to a national cup final. The author's opinion is that, if they could somehow play again in 2007, these players would simply adapt to modern training techniques and match preparation, and their inherent ability would secure them all a place at Championship level, which of course equates with the old Division Two.

Back at the start of the 1960/61 season, the same bunch of Rotherham United players who had played in 1959/60 assembled for pre-season training down at homely Millmoor. They had been together as a unit for several years, with several players resident at Millmoor from as far back as 1954/55, and the team was holding its own in Division Two. The new season's fixture list contained something different to play for, however, with a brand-new trophy to be contested. It was the inaugural competition for the Football League Cup.

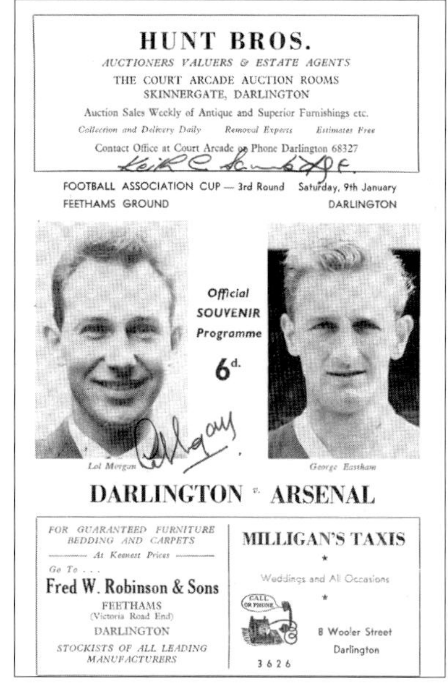

Darlington played Arsenal in a F.A. Cup 3rd Round tie on 9th January 1964. George Eastham (who is discussed in the adjoining text) played and is illustrated on the front cover of the match programme. Former Millers cup finalists Lol Morgan and Keith Bambridge both played for Darlington and have autographed the programme. (Adrian Booth collection)

3. The League Cup

Despite the new cup's existence on the 1960/61 season's fixture lists, the majority of football fans would actually be looking forward to the glamour of the famous F.A. Cup. The competition's first final was contested at the Kennington Oval on 16th March 1872 between The Wanderers and the Royal Engineers. The Wanderers won 1-0 before a crowd of some 2,000, all of whom would be blissfully unaware that they were witnessing the beginnings of a competition that would become an English institution and be followed all around the world. It grew to become a fabulously successful and much loved competition which was entered by all 92 League teams, plus literally hundreds of non-league teams that were affiliated to the F.A. (Football Association). From 1923 onwards the final was played at Wembley Stadium, the first being played in front of HM King George V. Bolton Wanderers beat West Ham United 2-0, witnessed by a crowd of 126,047, many of whom spilled on to the pitch and had to be cleared by a policeman and his famous white horse. Thereafter, many a famous final was fought out at Wembley, such as the well known 'Matthews Final' of 1953 and the 1961 final when Spurs completed the famous 'double'. It was (and still is) every non-league team's dream to fight their way to the competition's third round – at which point the bigger clubs enter – and receive an away draw at one of the game's giants, and so receive gate money which would at a stroke wipe out all the debts. It was almost a national institution to gather round the radio on Monday dinner time when the 3rd Round draw was broadcast live from F.A. headquarters.

The League Cup was an entirely different beast. It was the brainchild of Alan Hardaker, a well respected football administrator who was the Secretary of the Football League from 1957 to 1979. Hardaker had penned his radical 'Pattern for Football' whereby he suggested reducing the number of clubs to eighty, in four equal

Twenty-five players, two trainers, the club secretary, and manager Tom Johnston, pose for a traditional photograph prior to the start of the 1960/61 season. All were blissfully unaware that they were about to embark upon a run to a national cup final. Of the eleven players who were to represent the club in the final, ten are to be seen in this picture. The only absentee is Keith Bambridge who, being a part-time player, was presumably sat in his office whilst his team mates were all saying 'cheese'. (Graham Barnes collection)

divisions with four-up and four-down promotion and relegation. Obviously the fewer League games would have meant a decrease in annual club income, so Hardaker conceived a brand new cup competition to be played in mid-week. At the Annual Meeting of the Football League in May 1960, the 92 clubs (perhaps not unexpectedly) threw out Hardaker's master plan for a new League structure, but they liked the idea of a new cup competition which was approved by 31 votes to 16. Thus the League Cup was born in 1960/61, with only the 92 Football League sides qualifying to enter the new competition. Entry was optional in the early years, although it was made compulsory from 1971. Unlike the F.A. Cup, there was to be no seeding of the top sides until the 3rd Round, so every small club had a chance of getting a choice tie with one of the big boys. Additionally, in a bold move to create more interest – and income for the clubs – the semi-finals and final were scheduled to be fought out over two legs at the participants' grounds. Joe Richards, the chairman of Barnsley FC and President of the Football League from 1957 to 1966, purchased the silver trophy, which still bears his name. Alan Hardaker wrote: "Joe Richards was a small, dapper man, a tough old bird who learnt the business of life in the Yorkshire coalfields. His only language was honest Yorkshire but he seemed able to make himself understood no matter what country he was in. The impression he left was always lasting and favourable."

The inaugural competition suffered from apathy in certain self-styled elite quarters. Division One clubs Arsenal, Sheffield Wednesday, Tottenham Hotspur, West Bromwich Albion and Wolverhampton Wanderers refused to enter. Clearly these five misguided outfits did not share Hardaker's vision of generating cash for the smaller clubs. Possibly they took into account that the infant competition did not offer the prestige of a Wembley final, and thought it would create unwanted extra fixtures whilst they were competing at the top of the tree. Why run the risk, they possibly thought, of having to play a low key Football League Cup game versus Rochdale on a Monday night, when a First Division fixture versus Arsenal may be imminent? Officials of other clubs which did enter stated they thought that the competition was ill conceived and a burden on an already overcrowded season.

Despite these problems, the 1960/61 season saw the very first League Cup competition get underway and, of course, Rotherham United fought their way to the final. Crowds were generally poor, with the new cup competition slow to catch the public's imagination. The 1961/62 competition fared little better attendance wise, but little Rochdale had the last laugh on the big boys as they famously got through to the final. It was a significant finale, being the first major final not to feature a team from the top division. Rochdale (who finished the season twelfth in Division Four) lost to Norwich City (seventeenth in Division Two). The gradually improving stature of the competition meant that bigger teams started taking it more seriously – and winning it – and a new home was needed for the final. After six years of two-legged finals held at the finalists' grounds, the climax became a single game at Wembley with effect from 1966/67, when Third Division champions Queens Park Rangers stunned West Bromwich Albion (thirteenth in Division One) to win the cup in front of 97,952 fans in March 1967. West Bromwich Albion were winning 2-0 at half time but QPR (inspired by Rodney Marsh) staged a magnificent comeback to take the cup 3-2, causing one reporter to write: "Only in the delirium that followed England's World Cup triumph has Wembley witnessed the kind of wild enthusiasm that climaxed this astonishing triumph by the little team from Loftus Road." Alan Hardaker commented: "My thanks go to Alec Stock and his outstanding team. In 45 minutes they launched the League Cup." Thereafter all League Cup Finals were sell outs. Another famous final was in 1969 when Swindon Town of the Third Division toppled former abstainers, the mighty Arsenal, by 3-1 in another major upset.

It was noticeable that, when the competition had become established and the final was moved to Wembley, with the carrot dangled to the winners of qualifying for European competition, the old abstainers took the cup far more seriously! Hardaker it was who lobbied UEFA to win the right of European competition for the League Cup winners, with a result that a European Fairs Cup (later the UEFA Cup) place was up for grabs from the 1966/67 competition, with the proviso that the winners were a First Division side. In this era Hardaker quipped: "if the F.A. Cup is football's Ascot then the League Cup is its Derby Day." Sponsorship came onto the scene when the League Cup became the Milk Cup from 1981/82, the Littlewoods Challenge Cup from 1986/87, the Rumbelows League Cup from 1990/91, the Coca-Cola Cup from 1992/93, the Worthington Cup from 1998/99, and the Carling Cup from 2004. The venue for the final had to be changed from 2001, as Wembley was closed down for rebuilding, and the climax was moved to Cardiff.

4. Path to the First Final

The League Cup had a difficult birth and suffered from teething problems. This began with the draw for the 1st round, where the absence of the five abstaining clubs did not exactly help. In order that the second round would be reduced to 64 clubs, to facilitate a straight knock-out from that point onwards, some tinkering was in order. Thus no less than 41 clubs were drawn out of the hat to receive a first round bye: these included Yorkshire clubs Bradford City, Doncaster Rovers, Halifax Town, Huddersfield Town, Leeds United, Rotherham United, and Sheffield United. Other byes included Aston Villa and the now almost forgotten Workington. The remaining 46 clubs' balls went into the velvet bag, with the ultimate 23 winners scheduled to join the 41 byes to give 64 clubs for round two. The draw was then made, at the same meeting, for the second round of the competition. The first ever League Cup matches were played on Monday 26th September 1960 when Bristol Rovers beat Fulham 2-1, and West Ham United defeated Charlton Athletic by 3-1. The rest of the first round matches were subject to some chaotic scheduling, with the ties and replays eventually taking place between 26th September and Wednesday 26th October 1960. Some of the more interesting results included Colchester United's 4-1 victory over Newcastle United, Everton beating Accrington Stanley 3-1 at Goodison Park, Coventry City seeing off Barrow by 4-2, and Exeter City holding Manchester United 1-1 before losing out 1-4 in the replay at Old Trafford.

The chaotic nature was again in evidence as there was overlapping of the first two rounds with the average fan probably unsure of quite what was going on. The second round ties got underway on Wednesday 28th September 1960, precisely four weeks before the last first round ties were played, and only two days after the opening first round match! This came about because Leeds United and Blackpool had both been given byes in the first round, but knew they were meeting in the second, so they played their match on the first convenient date. Even this caused complications, because the sides drew 0-0 at Elland Road, and were forced to replay on Wednesday 5th October 1960, when Leeds United triumphed 3-1. Thus those opponents had played two second round ties before the first round was even completed! Second Round ties included Aston Villa progressing with a resounding 4-1 defeat of Huddersfield Town, Bradford Park Avenue losing at home to Birmingham City by one goal, Bradford City beating Manchester United 2-1, Chelsea beating Workington 4-2, and Bristol Rovers securing a fine away win by 5-3 at Reading. Altogether the second round stretched to Monday 14th November 1960 when Leyton Orient finally played Chesterfield, with the Spireites triumphing by the only goal of the game.

Rotherham United meanwhile made their League Cup debut on Wednesday 26th October 1960, having been drawn away to Leicester City. Founded in 1884 as Leicester Fosse, the club changed its name to Leicester City in 1919 and played at the well known Filbert Street ground. In 1960/61 City were a Division One club, having been promoted in 1956/57, and went on to finish that season in a creditable sixth position. They were also tough cup fighters in that era, reaching the F.A. Cup Final at Wembley in both season 1960/61 and 1962/63. Their side included goalkeeper Gordon Banks (who went on to become a world-class England international), and half backs Colin Appleton (later of Scarborough FC fame) and Frank McLintock. The Millers, who were then in Division Two, thus had a hard fight on their hands, but came away with an excellent 2-1 win, with Keith Kettleborough cementing a permanent place in Rotherham United history by scoring the Millers' first ever goal in the tournament.

The Leicester City match programme (price 4d) included on page 4 an item entitled 'Club Gossip'. This commented: "Tonight we are prepared for a very lively challenge, in the second round of the Football League Cup, from Second Division Rotherham. Already we have been given evidence of the interest in the new tournament, by many of the very satisfactory attendances for first and second round ties. There is no doubt of its appeal to followers of smaller clubs, for it brings that extra chance of a visit by a celebrated side. A group of First Division clubs have stayed outside the League Cup. We wonder whether the experiment will not be successful, and induce them to enter next season." On page 8 there was a welcome to the visitors which noted: 'That special brand of loyalty and enthusiasm that makes football such a great game has always been in evidence at Millmoor, headquarters of Rotherham United. In the face of heavy competition from the big guns of

Leicester City versus Rotherham United match programme on Wednesday 26th October 1960. This 2nd Round tie was the Millers first ever League Cup match. (Graham Barnes collection)

Sheffield, with their spacious terraces and imposing stands, Rotherham have achieved splendid results. They have had to hold their supporters strictly on merit, and it has been truly remarkable how the club has been able to thrive without receiving, or spending, vast sums. Without turning to the reference books, it is fairly safe to say that no other club has so consistently relied, in the main, on local material. At the hour of writing this, the composition of the Rotherham side against us is not certain, but there might well be nine players on view who were recruited from minor football in and around Rotherham. The entire defence unit could be players recruited locally."

The *Rotherham Advertiser* reporter was at the game and provided a detailed report of proceedings including Keith Kettleborough's now-famous goal. In its issue dated 29th October 1960 the newspaper recorded: "Although handicapped by an early injury to George Darwin, Rotherham United were the stronger and better team in their history making first ever Football League Cup tie at Filbert Street on Wednesday and were worthy 2-1 winners over Leicester City from Division 1. United were vivacious, eager and always determined in drizzle and clinging mud calculated to quickly sap the stamina of the fittest team. And it was a tribute to the fitness of the team that they finished in a much less fatigued state than Leicester. United skipper Roy Lambert said after the match that home players were sighing longingly for the final whistle ten minutes before it came. Rotherham showed us some attractive co-ordinated football and although the forwards had fewer clear-cut scoring chances than City it was the United forwards who got the goals – for a change. Leicester scored once and that goal came from a penalty kick. Ace of the floodlit battle was Keith Kettleborough, who played outstandingly well, back at inside forward after looking a shade out of touch at the beginning of the proceedings. But the other Keith – United's Keith Bambridge – played some brilliant football, leading fullback King a dizzy dance, and flitting over the balance shaking wet surface with such speed and ease that the ball sometimes looked as though it was tied to

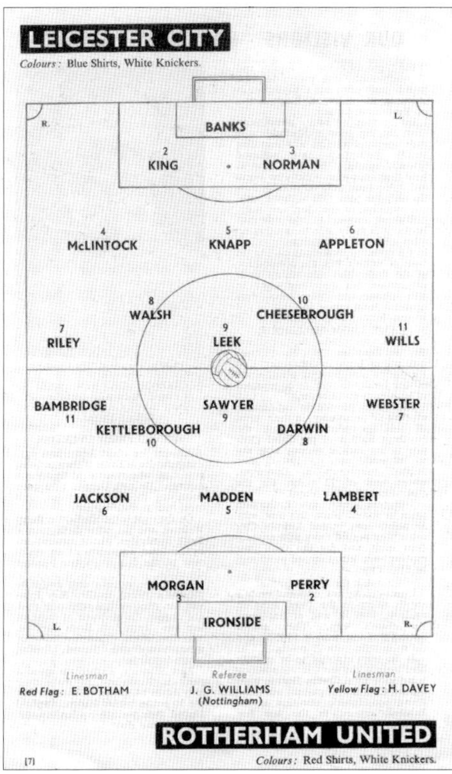

Team line-ups page from the Leicester City programme showing how, in those days, players were always depicted in the 1-2-3-5 formation. Even in 1960 the players' shorts were referred to as 'knickers'. George Darwin played number 8, his only appearance for the Millers in the competition. (Graham Barnes collection)

his boots. Bambridge gave the Leicester rearguard continuous trouble with his quicksilver darts and goalkeeper Banks must have been thankful that some of his scoring efforts were just on the wrong side of the woodwork. One admirable feature of United's play was the solidarity and glacier coolness of the defence, with placid and poised Lambert showing a fine example. There were times when the Rotherham captain brought the ball out of his own goalmouth to relieve pressure and to set his own attack moving with a level-headed deliberation that spoke volumes to me of soccer intelligence. Mark you, Lambert wasn't the only player to do this. So did Lol Morgan and Peter Perry. So did Peter Madden and Brian Jackson. Panic kicking would have been easy. It might also have been fatal. The ball was hard to move and it could have gone to the opposition. Lofty Madden was in commanding form and it is great to see him back in the number 5 shirt. And the man he displaced from the centre, the man who thought of a move because his future seemed so dim at Rotherham so long as Madden was there, played a splendid role as an attacking wing-half. Yes, Jackson did extraordinary well at left-half. Vivid memories are two first half bursts followed by two hard-hit drives which missed the Leicester goal by inches. Those were highlights, but Jackson's display as a whole impressed me. He played with a lot of skill, zest and determination. There must be a special pat on the back for goalkeeper Roy Ironside, who was always confidently safe and sometimes brilliant. Rotherham were a goal down at half time and we know full well that there are many occasions when the worst step opponents can take against a Rotherham team is to go in front. United often do better, and frequently show more resolution when they are behind than they do when they are in front and things are [*author's note*: due to the fragile condition of the original newspaper, part of the report is missing] vicious tackle which referee Mr J.G. Williams (Nottingham) ought to have foreseen and prevented. A foul was committed before this more serious one followed in its wake. Albert Wilson, the United trainer, had to carry Darwin to the touchline, but Darwin was soon back. Twelve minutes later, in the 32nd minute, Madden was caught on the wrong foot and as he threw in a desperate tackle Riley went over his outstretched right leg and sprawled in the penalty area. The upshot was a penalty. It was a harsh decision. King blasted the ball in from the spot. Ironside got his hand to the ball, but he could do no better than deflect it in to the corner of the net, so fast was it moving. United staged a great second half rally and they were undismayed by periods of Leicester pressure in which centre-forward Lornie put in a series of hard shots that were either stopped by Ironside or went flashing past the woodwork. Rotherham persistently played progressive football with an air of calm deliberation and this approach to the game brought its reward. With 20 minutes left, Sawyer centred from the right wing after Bambridge had sparked off an attack in his own half and Kettleborough slammed the ball into the roof of the net from short range. No player deserved to score more than he did. The winning goal came five minutes from the end when Darwin scored from Bambridge's centre. Although the home team gained several corners in the remaining time, the United defence refused to be broken. Teams; Leicester City: Banks; King, Norman; McLintock, Knapp, Appleton; Riley, Walsh, Lornie, Cheesborough, Wills. Rotherham United: Ironside; Perry, Morgan; Lambert, Madden, Jackson; Webster, Darwin, Sawyer, Kettleborough, Bambridge." The attendance was 6,244. Albert Wilson is mentioned in the report and is remembered as a loyal servant of Rotherham United, spending over thirty years at Millmoor as a player, trainer (from 1952) and groundsman (from 1968). Older supporters will remember Albert (with distinctive hat) out on the pitch at half time at every match with a small team of youngsters, each with a long handled fork, repairing divots.

Meanwhile, in its issue dated 27th October 1960, the *Sheffield Star* contained a shorter report, written by John Piper: "A first half penalty goal for Leicester failed to upset Rotherham United in their second round League Cup tie at Leicester. Having overcome an early second half danger period, when City were shooting hard and often, the Yorkshire men seized victory with two fine goals. Kettleborough, back in the forward line like a colossus, rammed home Sawyer's long pass with easy surety, and Darwin, at very reduced power because of an injury, registered the winner after Bambridge had lined it up with brilliant ball play, five minutes from time. Leicester won corner after corner in the last stages of the game but United knew exactly where they were going and were in no danger. In the end, Rotherham were much the classier side. If there was a difference in the early part it lay in Rotherham's greater concentration and Leicester's shooting power in all five forward places. All the time, the Rotherham defenders were tightening their grip, making their opponents shoot from longer and longer range in the rain and mud. Whenever there was a breakthrough, Ironside's goalkeeping after two slips was superb. Among the game's most happy features was the contribution of Jackson at wing half. Cultured in his use of the ball, he might have had a goal with a 25 yard shot. Sawyer was a trifle rusty and out of touch after weeks in the reserves. Knapp is highly uncompromising at centre half but when Sawyer moved on to the wing, and Webster switched for fetching and carrying duty, the Leicester left defensive flank was frequently in difficulty. On the other wing, Bambridge persistently irritated King. King shot Leicester's penalty goal given when Madden brought down Riley."

The *Sheffield Star* mentioned how Keith Bambridge, with some brilliant ball play, lined up the winning goal for the injured George Darwin. Speaking on 30th July 2005 Keith recalled: "George Darwin was quite badly injured and we later discovered that he had torn his cartilages. During my own career I suffered this identical injury and can state that it is extremely painful. The very fact that George stayed on the pitch was courage personified for he played in great pain. [No substitutes were permitted in that era.] After his injury, manager Tom Johnston asked George to play at centre forward, the tactic being that the ball could be played up to him and he could lay it off in either direction to wherever there was a supporting player. His presence meant that Leicester City's centre half had to keep a careful watch on him. For the winning goal, George had managed to

A gang of men engaged in erecting the new floodlights at Millmoor in 1960. The concrete wall on the right, together with the building behind it, formed an enclosed narrow alleyway along which the players had to walk between the Players' Entrance and the changing rooms that were located beneath the grandstand (seen in the right background). This alleyway was always Mecca for autograph hunters who thus had a good 50 or 60 yards in which to cajole their heroes to sign pictures and autograph books! (Adrian Booth collection)

Rotherham United versus Bristol Rovers programme, for the 3rd Round match played under floodlights on Wednesday 23rd November 1960. (Graham Barnes collection)

take up a good position and I heard him shouting. I passed the ball to him and he hit it in."

The Third Round got underway on Monday 14th November 1960 when three ties were played, including Norwich City winning 4-1 away at Derby County. The following night Preston North End fought out a 3-3 draw with visiting Aston Villa, with the replay on the 23rd seeing Villa winning 3-1. On the 16th Doncaster Rovers crashed spectacularly at home to Chelsea who scored seven without reply. The sixteen ties were completed on Tuesday 6th December 1960 when Burnley beat Brentford 2-1 in a replay at Turf Moor.

Rotherham United's third round tie took place on Wednesday 23rd November 1960, when they played Bristol Rovers at Millmoor. Rovers are traditionally the poor relations of their more illustrious City rivals, but were then an established Division Two side, having been promoted as Third Division (South) champions in 1952/53. In season 1960/61 they finished in seventeenth position in Division Two, then being based at their old home of the Eastville Ground. They fell from grace at the end of season 1961/62, being relegated to Division Three. Remembering the cup tie, Alan Kirkman recalls that: "the game has a special place in Millers history. We beat Bristol Rovers 2-0 in the first senior match to be played at Millmoor under the newly installed floodlights. There had been a reserve match versus Darlington two days earlier, but this was the first team's opener. It is difficult to convey to younger fans how exciting floodlit football was in those days. We had been used to Millmoor without the lights, 6pm kick-offs for evening games, and 2-15pm for winter Saturdays and mid-week afternoons for cup replays – and then there came the big expansion of floodlights into the lower division grounds. The spectacle was simply out of this world, and to we young players the lights seemed so bright. We certainly shone that night and on we went to round 4."

The Rotherham United match programme (price 3d) emphasised the historic occasion with the front cover proclaiming: 'Kick Off 7.15 p.m. – Floodlight Match'. On the inside cover the Secretary's telephone number was shown as Rotherham 2434, which is quite a comparison with modern multi-digit numbers. Adverts within the issue included those of Ben Bennett Junior Ltd, the Rickshaw Restaurant on Wellgate, Wm. Varah – haulage contractor of Wickersley, the Olde Gayte Café on Wellgate, and the Rotherham Surgical Company – stockists of reliable surgical goods. The programme editor remarked: “The Football League Cup, newest of the major competitions in English soccer, has had a veritable array of critics since its introduction. Some clubs, feeling that the match schedules are sufficiently cluttered up, have stayed outside the event. The majority of attendances at the ties that have so far been played cannot be said to have been encouraging, though tit-bit games – like the visit of Chelsea to Doncaster's Belle Vue last week – have had very good reception. Of course, for the lesser brothers of the League, the great attraction, outside the down to earth cash reasons, are the chances of a star opposition being landed at home. Our second round game with Leicester City did not carry very much value financially and, incidentally, carried a very high price with the injury to George Darwin. But we had a most enjoyable game of football, deserving to beat opponents who on the same home ground last Saturday accounted for Sheffield Wednesday. [19th November 1960] Bristol Rovers come here tonight as bottom of the table for the first time in their 2nd Division career which began at the start of the 1954/55 season [it was actually 1953/54] ... Yes, these days are difficult ones for Bert Tann. This much is certain. There will be a team of triers and fighters from the West Country.”

The *Rotherham Advertiser* dated 26th November 1960 provided a lengthy report on the Bristol Rovers game: “For Rotherham United, passage to the fourth round of the Football League Cup was merely a formality. They had to go through the procedure of eliminating an inept Bristol Rovers side on Wednesday in their first senior team match under the Millmoor floodlights. Their 2-0 win was infinitely more comfortable than it appears in the light of the final score and the Rovers were sent away from Rotherham without getting a goal for the second time this season, having already lost 4-0 in the Second Division. As an attacking unit, the Rovers were rarely in the reckoning at all. So if you think United are weak within shooting range – and, by jove, they are – sympathise with Bert Tann, the Bristol manager. He's got much more to worry about than his Rotherham counterpart, Tom Johnston. Tann's team find it difficult to even plan their way to firing range. The Rovers were jolly lucky to escape with only a two goal beating. They did not do as badly as they ought to have done and for this they can thank busy goalkeeper Radford, who made some fine saves, a defence which often packed solidly in the penalty area, the largely ineffective finishing of the home forwards, and a fair slice of good fortune. The ball went into the Bristol net twice – three times if you count the effort of Brian Sawyer, who was ruled offside by the referee, Mr J. Kelly of Chorley. But it should have gone in at least six times. All the United forwards – yes, all the five – missed scoring chances. Alan Kirkman and Sawyer passing up at least one ‘sitter’ apiece and Eddie O'Hara wasting two heaven sent opportunities. O'Hara, who could have made the Rovers defenders shiver in their boots, twice fired weakly past the woodwork with his right foot when all he had to do was pick the spots for Radford to retrieve the ball from. United proved again that they have the skill and intelligence up front to create their goal chances, but it was amazing that only two goals resulted from their overwhelming territorial superiority. Ultimately, Rovers looked incapable of scoring, for there was an awful lot of looseness in the United defence at times, particularly at full back, and the Bristol attack was able to find big gaps in Rotherham territory in which to build up approach work. Fortunately, however, the Bristol forwards were not good enough to take advantage of the rope they were allowed before the United defence really put the screws in. Against a better side Rotherham could have been in deep water as the minutes ticked by, and the chances went with them. They owed a debt to centre half Peter Madden – fit to play after doubts caused by a cold – who played a classy role, dominating the middle and sometimes snuffing out threats of trouble on the flanks too. Skipper Roy Lambert was in much improved form as well, more like the shrewd and clever wing half we respect. These two players were United's outstanding defenders. Ken Houghton, turning out again at inside right, impresses more and more with every game he plays. He looked confident and he played a thoughtful, strong brand of soccer, capping his display with a powerfully cracked goal, his 24th in his first season of professional football and his third for the first team. Experience in the Football League will make him a player for defences to know and mark well. Kirkman, though obviously still very conscious of that so recently healed broken foot, showed occasional bursts of menacing speed on the wing, and Sawyer although fulfilment was not equal to promise, was always a potential danger. If only he could produce the scoring edge which earned him something of a reputation as a marksman last season when he grabbed some brilliant goals! Keith Kettleborough and O'Hara were patchy. Kettleborough mixed the good with the bad in his distribution and his shooting was dreadful. O'Hara disappointed to the point of exasperation after cleverly preparing his way to the target area and finishing so innocuously. Radford began his valuable work for Bristol in the second minute when he somehow kept out a fast drive from Houghton and Rovers might easily have had a penalty given against them when a ball from Sawyer on the right wing was handled, perhaps involuntarily by Pyle. My notebook shows that Rovers brought goalkeeper Roy Ironside into action twice in 18 minutes and the fact that centre forward Geoff Bradford cleared off the Bristol goal line gives some indication of the heat United turned on. Then left full back Watling cleared off the line and Radford was in action continually, often stopping the ball through the intentional exercise of his skill and agility and sometimes keeping the ball out with the aid of a little good luck. Houghton, thwarted in the early minutes, suffered frustration again when Radford brilliantly turned his swift, close range header behind with his finger tips, via the crossbar, and just before half time Kirkman missed a good chance to put United ahead from close quarters. A minute after the resumption, Rotherham took the lead. No wonder Houghton jumped for joy after slamming the ball in when it came loose to his feet in the penalty area following a Sawyer centre which the Bristol defence failed to get away. Veteran Bradford missed a golden equaliser chance, the sort of opportunity he would rarely have missed in his younger days and that was Bristol's swansong. Sawyer lost an easy chance to inscribe his name on the scoresheet, but Kirkman made it 2-0 two minutes from the end after earlier failing to beat Radford to a bad back pass. Kettleborough shot and the ball bounced off a defender to the United winger who hit the ball home quickly. Rotherham United: Ironside; Perry, Morgan; Lambert, Madden, Waterhouse; Kirkman, Houghton, Sawyer, Kettleborough, O'Hara. Bristol Rovers: Radford; Hillard, Watling; Sykes, Pyle, Mabbutt; Petheridge, Biggs, Bradford, Ward, Hooper." The attendance was 10,912.

Writing in the *Sheffield Star* dated 24th November 1960, John Piper reported: "Howard Radford, the super agile Bristol Rovers goalkeeper, has consistently covered himself in match glory on his several visits to Millmoor. He did it again in the third round League Cup tie under the new floodlights and finished beaten on only two occasions. Sometimes in the furious goalmouth incidents, he was a little lucky. He deserved every scrap of it. But the fact is that he should have been reflecting on at least another four and quite easily seven or eight goals past him if the weight of Rotherham's shooting opportunities is to be a yard string. There were only two occasions in the entire pleasant and hard working game when the West Country side looked likely to score. The general ingredients of the United team were substantially better than in the last three League matches and young Ken Houghton had clearly his most authoritative and impressive game so far. Some of his ball control and thoughtful distribution wore an air of very great inside experience when in fact he is only half a dozen matches old in the Second Division. With Bristol there seems to be so little combined thinking and method; their plotting was not suitable; yet with the naked evidence of the first half, they persisted in its perpetration. The return of Alan Kirkman, quite apart from being a tribute to a remarkably quick fitness recovery after a broken foot, was very useful, in spite of the fact he missed the easiest chance of the game. Peter Madden followed his good game at Bramall Lane with an impeccable performance. Ken Waterhouse came back quietly but effectively, and Roy Lambert had a delightful game at wing half once Dai Ward had been crushed out of the proceedings."

The Fourth Round saw the inaugural competition's last sixteen clubs in the draw. Two of the round's eight ties were played before the Third Round's final replay, on Monday 5th December 1960, and included a thrilling all Division Two tussle at The Dell where Southampton beat Leeds United 5-4. After their excellent results in the previous round, two clubs went out together on Wednesday 14th December 1960 when Chelsea lost 0-1 away at Portsmouth and Norwich City lost by the same score away at Shrewsbury Town. Aston Villa's tie with Plymouth Argyle turned into a marathon, starting with a 3-3 draw at Villa Park on Tuesday 13th December 1960. The replay in Devon was held on Monday 19th December 1960 and ended goalless. It was not until Monday 6th February 1961 that the second replay could be fitted in (again at Plymouth) when Villa came away with a thrilling 5-3 victory.

Rotherham United had been given another tough away draw and, on Tuesday 20th December 1960 they travelled over the Pennines to take on Bolton Wanderers at Burnden Park having, for the second time in the competition, been drawn away at a Division One club. Bolton Wanderers were founder members of the Football League in 1888 and were one of the many famous Lancastrian clubs which played regularly in top flight football. Indeed, Bolton had enjoyed uninterrupted Division One status since before World War 2 and consequently the Wanderers' match programme (price 3d) noted: "Club history is made this evening with the visit of Rotherham United: it is the first time we have met the Yorkshire club in any competition. To all our visitors we extend hearty greetings on their initial appearance at Burnden Park." The Millers accepted the hearty greetings, but were not deterred by their host's pedigree and higher status and came home with a lovely Christmas present in the form of a superb 2-0 win. Bolton Wanderers finished eighteenth in Division One that season, but finally lost their top flight status at the end of season 1963/64.

In its issue dated Friday 23rd December 1960, the *Rotherham Advertiser* reported: "Victory over Bolton Wanderers by 2-0 on their first visit to Burnden Park, gave Rotherham United a ticket for passage to the quarter finals of the Football League Cup on Tuesday. In the first instance, it was a fourth round win that seemed unlikely. Then it became a possible success. And finally, with the first goal, just under half an hour from the end, a Rotherham triumph became a certainty. Initially, United were tentative and unsure in their approach to the game, despite the tremendous financial incentives of £10 bonus plus £3 appearance money, for the winners. Perhaps the absence of Peter Madden, often the towering figure at centre half and the master of the middle, who was unable to play because of a cold, had an adverse psychological effect before the team realised their luck was in, found their feet, and really settled to their task. And, of course, the opposition was new too and settling down thus posed fresh problems for Rotherham. The uneasiness of the early stages was reflected in defensive shakiness and the failure of Alan Kirkman to score from an easy chance in the eighth minute. But the soccer Gods were with Rotherham in this crisis period and they emerged from it unscathed. Gradually they made a Bolton team which became too readily dispirited look decidedly second best. They shook off the nervousness and got on top, with their defence looking assured and their forwards confident in carving their way to goal. In fact, United were so superior in the final stages although Bolton were only a single goal in arrears, that red shirted players were sometimes able to stroll along with the ball. United's determination to win through to the last eight in the competition squeezed all the fight out of the Wanderers, the side with the reputation for toughness. Obviously the absence of Nat Lofthouse, injured last Saturday at Birmingham, was more serious to Bolton than the absence of Madden was to Rotherham. Brian Jackson proved a capable enough deputy for Madden, but he is not the same commanding player in the air as United's regular centre half, as supporters know well, and Bolton slipped up in not exploiting this Rotherham weakness properly. Their centre forward, Bill McAdams, is tall and potentially an extremely dangerous leader in the air, yet Wanderers invariably kept the ball close on the ground in the middle of Rotherham territory and it was at ground level that Jackson excelled. Two players in the United team I would pick out for special mention are full back Lol Morgan, who undoubtedly made victory ultimately possible for his side with his clearances when all seemed lost, and centre forward Brian Sawyer, for my money the best forward on the field in a worrying, roving, hard-working way. Bolton manager Bill Ridding and the directors were impressed by Sawyer's form and I wouldn't be surprised if Wanderers' interest in the United

BOLTON WANDERERS FOOTBALL CLUB

BURNDEN PARK, BOLTON

SEASON 1960-61

DIRECTORS: C. N. BANKS (Chairman), Ald. J. ENTWISTLE, J.P. (Vice-Chairman), W. HAYWARD, E. GERRARD, J.P., H. WARBURTON, J. BATTERSBY, H. T. TYLDESLEY

Manager-Secretary: W. RIDDING

Telephone: BOLTON 800. Telegrams: "WANDERERS, BOLTON."

FOOTBALL LEAGUE CUP—4th ROUND

Tuesday, December 20th

WANDERERS v. ROTHERHAM UNITED

OFFICIAL PROGRAMME 3D.

***Right.* Bolton Wanderers versus Rotherham United programme, for the 4th Round match played on Tuesday 20th December 1960. Brian Sawyer recalls that it was in this game that the Millers played their best football in the competition. (Adrian Booth collection)**

man is renewed in a very positive sort of way. Of course, Bolton are also keenly interested in Madden, but they were denied the opportunity of another look at him this time on their own ground. With all the goal to aim at, Kirkman fired wide of the far post from the inside right position in the eighth minute after Sawyer had laid on a chance for him. Fiddling by Waterhouse and Morgan enabled McAdams to gain possession, but, fortunately for United, his hard hit drive cannoned behind off the angle of crossbar and upright. Then Roy Ironside was caught a shade too far out of his goal by a terrific shot from Rimmer, but his long reach saved the day and he strained to turn the ball over the bar. Rotherham were lucky when Morgan ballooned the ball high and it was carried backwards by the strong downfield wind. Jackson failed to clear when the ball came out of orbit and Deakin seized it and fired in a drive which hit Ironside's knees as the goalkeeper came out. The Bolton onslaught continued with United's biggest slice of good fortune of the night. A shot from Birch was deflected on to a post by Morgan's foot. The ball was behind Ironside but he had the presence of mind to spin round and pick it up before it rolled over the goal line. At this early stage of the match, the Rotherham defenders were bemused by Bolton's fast, menacing thrusts. They held off the tackle and retreated and generally behaved as though they were expecting a thrashing. Having helped to save Rotherham's goal from downfall once, Morgan stepped in again for the saviour's role when he took the ball off the toes of Deakin and headed away the resultant corner kick. Between their perilous adventures in defence, United put in some useful raids and it was their turn to grumble about hard luck when Keith Bambridge laid on a shooting chance with a peach of a square pass to Ken Houghton and the inside left's characteristically hard shot smacked against the bottom of England goalkeeper Hopkinson's left hand post, with the keeper himself nowhere near the ball. United's task was made easier by a knee injury to Bolton's centre half John Higgins, a sturdy, often impassable individual and one of Wanderers key men in their 1958 F.A. Cup Final win. He limped along in the forward line for the last 10 minutes of the first half and a big part of the second half before returning to his proper position. Morgan thwarted Bolton again when he cleared a shot from Birch off the goal line to prevent an otherwise inevitable goal, but Birch shot straight at advancing Ironside just before half time after bursting through and getting a great goal chance. Houghton must speed up his football. If he had been quicker he might have scored soon after the resumption. Bambridge gave Hopkinson something to think about with a wickedly in swinging ball from the left which the goalkeeper had to turn on to the top of the goal netting and United then got a lucky goal. Bambridge centred and Houghton should have taken the ball and scored with comfort, but he missed it and for some unknown reason left full back Farrimond got himself into a terrible tangle, although unchallenged in trying to get the ball away, and put it into his own net. That bit of luck – in the 62nd minute – was the break Rotherham had been looking for and it took practically all the stuffing out of Bolton. Confident United gave them a hammering. Sawyer put through Kirkman and Hopkinson made a great save from his point blank drive; Kirkman headed just over the top and Sawyer tested Hopkinson with a header and a shot. In a last desperate attempt to equalise, Wanderers forced a corner and there was a short, but hectic, scramble around the Rotherham goal which ended with the ball being cleared. With three minutes left, Houghton fired the final fatal round at Bolton and their hopes. Kirkman left him with a clear cut shooting chance with a perfect through pass and he hit the ball confidently past the helpless Hopkinson. Bolton: Hopkinson; Hartle, Farrimond; Stanley, Higgins, Rimmer; Birch, Stevens, McAdams, Deakin, Hender. Rotherham: Ironside; Perry, Morgan; Lambert, Jackson, Waterhouse; Webster, Kirkman, Sawyer, Houghton, Bambridge. Referee: Mr J.K. Taylor (Wolverhampton). Attendance: 6,594."

John Piper provided his usual report in the *Sheffield Star* dated 21st December 1960, noting: "Whatever may be the limitations of the first season of the Football League Cup and however hard the 'knockers' work on it, Rotherham United are enjoying themselves. Now in the last eight, they have beaten two First Division clubs away from home and Bristol Rovers from their own section of the League at Millmoor. Bolton – surely the most muddled, stricken Wanderers for many years – last night went the way of Leicester with defeat on their own ground. Failing to take some first half chances, and baulked by some good defensive play in other instances, Bolton ought to have had more to show from a bright start. But Houghton, who finally scored one of his bomb goals, on the run, had hit a post and Kirkman had missed appallingly. The early story was turned upside down and we had Bolton in lots of defensive trouble and quite inadequate in all three of their inside forward positions. The wing promise had been wiped out by Morgan and Perry as Lambert and Waterhouse soccer strangled the inside men. Sometimes in some places there was not enough courage or effort by Wanderers even allowing for the part game injury of Higgins. Once they were behind to Farrimond's own goal they were a beaten side. More of the spirit and ability of former Rotherham schoolboy Graham Stanley would have been handy for them. Mostly they preferred the quicker stuff, played on the short pass, and Brian Jackson at number five took all of it in educated stride. Brian Sawyer was again the most diligent and skilful attacker. Bolton native Alan Kirkman missed an early chance to get himself a home town goal. Rotherham's five forward attacking plan, whilst still subject to amendment and development, is proving attractive and encouraging. Ken Houghton injured his knee in the match but is expected to be fit for the Christmas games against Liverpool."

Things were beginning to get interesting, for the Millers were through to the competition's last eight clubs. The four quarter finals were all played on different dates. On Monday 6th February 1961, Southampton lost 2-4 at home to Burnley. On Wednesday 15th February 1961, Shrewsbury Town (of Division Three) caused something of a sensation when they entertained Everton (who finished fifth in Division One) and sent them back to Merseyside with a stinging 2-1 defeat. After needing three replays to get through the previous two rounds, Aston Villa made sure of further progress in convincing fashion: on Wednesday 22nd February 1961 they beat lowly Division Four side Wrexham by 3-0.

Rotherham United were drawn at home to Portsmouth, the fabled 'Pompey' of historic Division One pedigree, but who were relegated from Division Two at the end of 1960/61. (They came straight back up as Division Three champions in 1961/62.) Portsmouth travelled up from their well known Fratton Park home in Hampshire for the match on Monday 13th February 1961, which kicked off at 7-30pm under the new floodlights. Portsmouth's side included the famous Jimmy Dickinson, a clean tackling player with fine distribution, who was one of the most loyal one-club players of all time, clocking up a staggering 764 League matches for Pompey between 1946 and 1965. Dickinson won the first of his 48 full international England caps in May 1949. Renowned for his immaculate manners both on and off the pitch – never once booked – he was universally known as 'Gentleman Jim'. Rotherham United were in no mood to give any favours to Dickinson, however, and sent Pompey home after a 3-0 thrashing.

The Rotherham United match programme (price 3d) included the Editor's note that: "A few days ago one of the game's leading administrators on a brief visit to Rotherham observed that the new Football League Cup competition was virtually a waste of time and likely to be scrapped after a season or two. He also suggested that neither players nor spectators were very interested. One might – as indeed I did – commend him to seeking the views of some of the players still in the event on the one hand, and to note some of the attendances when big clubs have met little 'uns on the other. Those least interested in the new event are either those not participating therein, or those who have been eliminated at an early stage. As far as Rotherham are concerned we are very interested indeed in the competition, and with away successes against Leicester City and Bolton Wanderers to our credit have reaped considerable experience. No one ever imagined that the League Cup would immediately equal or oust the time honoured Football Association Cup in soccer affections. It was introduced as a subsidiary means of helping to raise funds for the lesser brothers of the League. Those clubs who have scorned the competition might well do worse than give that a further thought for next season. Of course it has not been the immediate money-spinner one would have wished, but there have been signs that with better planning next term the League Cup can be a most worthwhile innovation."

The *Rotherham Advertiser* dated 18th February 1961 reported: "Quicksilver Don Weston sent Rotherham United easily into the semi finals of the Football League Cup at Millmoor on Monday. Portsmouth could not restrain the alert, dashingly irrepressible home team leader, who had them spinning to inevitable defeat by half time, hitting two goals himself and laying on another for Houghton. I had heard Rotherham criticised for paying out their biggest ever fee for a player who was supposed to add punch to the forward line and who had failed to do so. But I did not hear that particular kind of criticism on Monday when Weston returned to centre forward from inside forward because Sawyer, leader and scorer in the previous two [League] matches was unfit. Weston's match winning performance, his scoring feats, gave that large transfer tag a fully justified look, but it was obvious from the start of the ex-Birmingham player's career at Rotherham, in my reiterated opinion, that a winner had been signed. Weston is fast, mentally and physically, eager for goals, and so adaptable that he is capable of playing anywhere in the front line. Name the attack position and he will fill it adequately. He has already played at centre forward and in both inside forward positions for

Rotherham United versus Portsmouth programme, for the 5th Round match played on Monday 13th February 1961. (Graham Barnes collection)

Rotherham and he was used successfully as a winger by Birmingham. The general standard of the game was undermined because United were not extended. Rotherham soon took control. They were ahead quickly and led 3-0 by half time. Portsmouth, twice First Division champions since the War, and once F.A. Cup winners, were not good enough to test the skill and power of a clever and confident – almost cocky and impertinent – Rotherham side and the second half was predominantly negative and boring as the relentless aggression of the first period was relaxed and United took it easy. United's willingness to leave the goals margin at 3-0 saved some face for weak, disheartened Portsmouth, who probably only see victory in these lean days when they visit their home town's dockyard, but it was hardly fair on the 11,918 paying spectators who wanted more goals and some entertainment from men in a winning team receiving £15 apiece for ninety minutes football. Nevertheless, it was worth going to the match just to see Weston's goals, particularly his first, which was thrilling and spectacular. Weston himself laid on the first goal for Houghton. In the 12th minute he put a perfect through pass down the centre for the inside left who fired the ball low into the right hand corner of the net, past the diving goalkeeper Beattie, with a shot that had a somewhat miss-hit look about it. This was Houghton's 28th goal as a professional, his eighth for the first team, and his third League Cup bulls-eye. United, 1-0 up, already had a composed winning appearance, but Weston really scuttled Portsmouth with two great goals in six minutes. The first came in the 36th minute and I cannot remember seeing a goal to equal this one for sheer power and spot on accuracy. Weston collected a loose ball about forty yards out, beat two men and thumped the ball with his right foot from 25 yards or so. In a flash it was in the right hand corner of the Portsmouth net and Beattie must have felt like a target at the wrong end of a rifle range. I think that drive would have outwitted better goalkeepers than Beattie. After a taste of Weston's nasty extra strong shooting medicine, Portsmouth received a fatal dose of his speed in the forty second minute. Webster, brought back at outside right in a reshuffle caused by Sawyer's injury, pushed the ball down the centre and Weston was through Portsmouth's square defence like a hare and slipping the ball past advancing Beattie into the net before the visitors could turn round. With 48 minutes of the match left, it was all over bar the yawning and I will draw a dark impenetrable veil over Pompey's pathetic scoring efforts of the second period as Rotherham let them have a little rope in attack. Even allowing for Rotherham's generosity, Portsmouth had some narrow escapes at their own end and were lucky not to bid the League Cup a more humiliating farewell. Between now and next Saturday, when they play at Millmoor again, this time in a Second Division match, Portsmouth will no doubt be wondering what they can do to suppress Weston and Houghton and solve the problem of that unyielding Rotherham defence, which treated their feeble forward line almost contemptuously at times. I am glad the problem isn't mine for the tackling and I'll bet Freddie Cox is glad it isn't his too. Remember him? He was Portsmouth's manager until he and the club parted company last week. Rotherham United: Ironside; Perry, Morgan; Lambert, Madden, Waterhouse; Webster, Kirkman, Weston, Houghton, Bambridge. Portsmouth: Beattie; Rutter, Dickinson; Howells, Gunter, Harris; Priscott, Chapman, White, Blackburn, Campbell. Referee: Mr A.W. Sparling (Grimsby)."

Meanwhile, John Piper filed his usual piece in the *Sheffield Star* and, in the issue dated Tuesday 14th February 1961, wrote: "I've seen the great majority of the 1,178 League goals scored by Rotherham since the War, but Don Weston's first and the team's second in the floodlit League Cup quarter final at Millmoor goes straight into the best dozen ever. It was the complete and perfect twenty five yard shot in soccer's proverbial right hand corner. More than that, it was prepared with a brilliant flash of ball play. And following on Ken Houghton's first goal it doomed Portsmouth to beginning their ride to a seventh defeat in a row. Weston got another goal – this the reward for his remarkable acceleration – as he streaked onto a Webster pass. It was moaned about for offside, but Portsmouth had no grounds. That in forty two minutes was the end of the scoring and more or less the end of the game, simply because we had been so feasted that the remainder was like a bread and water diet. In all conscience it was pretty bare stuff, with United failing badly to build up a goal aggregate which in their four League Cup ties is 9-1 in their favour. Later still, Portsmouth engaged Ironside twice, and the large size Portsmouth defensive line of Dickinson, Gunter and Rutter were strong enough on the ground. On the turn and on the chase they were mostly untidy and insufficient. They need more craft as well as power at half back. Webster, returning to the team, tried frantically hard and was very unfortunate not to get a goal just before the finish. Bambridge, with plenty of the ball, was disappointing after his marked improvement in the Scunthorpe match. But trace the real heart of this Rotherham success to the half back division of Lambert, Madden and Waterhouse, with Weston the outstanding forward. If I was looking for a promising young winger, Priscott, aged 19, the Pompey number seven – until he lost heart – would do nicely. Incidentally, the next home League match for Rotherham is Portsmouth, on Saturday week." [25th February 1961, when Rotherham won 1-0.]

By now things were getting very interesting indeed for Rotherham United, who were through to the last four! The semi finals were to be played over two legs at the participants' grounds. The teams who had made it through were Division One clubs Burnley and Aston Villa, Division Two Rotherham United and Division Three Shrewsbury Town. No offence to the Shrews, but there was no doubt who the other three teams were hoping to draw! Luck was on the Millers side. When the draw was made the two senior clubs were paired together, and the Millers were left with the relatively easier task of overcoming Shrewsbury Town in order to progress to the first ever final. Could the Millers do it? Excitement grew around the town. The League Cup competition may have started out as an unknown quantity, played before small gates, but when the semi final had been reached it suddenly took on a whole new importance. On Monday 10th April 1961 the first division clubs met at Turf Moor and fought out a 1-1 draw. The second leg was held at Villa Park on Wednesday 26th April 1961 and again ended up as a draw, this time 2-2. A decider was therefore necessary and, held on Tuesday 2nd May 1961 at Manchester United's Old Trafford stadium, resulted in Aston Villa winning 2-1. The Midlands side thus triumphed 5-4 on aggregate and were through to the final. Who would their opponents be?

Rotherham United's first leg semi final match was played at Millmoor on Tuesday 21st March 1961, kick-off at 7pm, with the Millers entertaining Shrewsbury Town. United beat Town 3-2, including a brace of Brian Sawyer goals. The Shropshire side were relative newcomers to senior football, only having entered the League in 1950/51 when the competition was expanded from 88 to 92 clubs. Based at their Gay Meadow stadium on the banks of the River Severn (their home since 1910), Shrewsbury Town were a Division Three side that finished 1960/61 in tenth position. Their side included the famous forward

Rotherham United versus Shrewsbury Town programme, in the first leg of the semi final on Tuesday 21st March 1961. (Graham Barnes collection)

Arthur Rowley, the highest goal scorer in League football history who scored 434 goals in 619 League games between 1946 and 1965. He notched four goals for West Bromwich Albion, 27 for Fulham, 251 for Leicester City (1950-58), 152 for Shrewsbury Town and, when he hung up his boots, Rowley had become the only player to have scored twenty goals or more in thirteen successive seasons.

The Millers' match programme (price 3d) contained notes from the Editor who wrote: "Welcome to the first ever semi-final of the Football League Cup competition. When the competition was launched at the beginning of this season – among considerable misgivings and on some hands indifference – our most devoted fans could hardly have contemplated United as semi-finalists. Now we are within just two games of the first final and with the greatest of respect to our Shropshire lads, possessing a very good chance of meeting the winners of the Villa-Burnley tie. ... In considering the chances of reaching the final tie most people will agree that a two-match basis favours the higher quality club. It also has the virtue of presenting a specially attractive game to both sets of home fans. ... For myself I imagine that the players would have preferred to play first at Shrewsbury. That way you know exactly how you stand for the second leg. It is probably true to say that United must look for a win to the tune of at least three clear goals if they are to travel to Shrewsbury in eight days time feeling their place in the final is assured. Against Everton on their own ground in the previous round the Town looked a very useful side, in the view of manager Tom Johnston and chief scout Mark Hooper. There is no under-estimating the standards of tonight's visitors. ... The individual cash rewards are high for players. The prestige is at stake. ... Winning through to the final is of very great importance, creating as it assuredly does, extra colourful interest at a time in the season when public enthusiasm is pretty low."

The *Rotherham Advertiser* dated 25th March 1961 reported: "Disappointment in victory may seem illogical, but that must have been the reaction of Rotherham United supporters at Millmoor on Tuesday, after the home team's 3-2 League Cup semi final (first leg) win over resolute Shrewsbury Town. Most of the 13,397 spectators at Millmoor, for this history making first League Cup semi final in English football, must have expected a more clear-cut United win and a wider credit goals margin to start the second leg at Shrewsbury next Wednesday evening. United certainly should have built up a decisive lead. As it is they have only a one goal advantage with a game to come at Gay Meadow, where an all-ticket near 20,000 crowd will be roaring their heads off to encourage Shrewsbury into the final. Missed scoring chances – a constantly recurring phrase in Rotherham soccer writing – some very fine goalkeeping by Mike Gibson, a bit of luck for Shrewsbury, the sheer determination of the visitors. United's fatal defensive looseness, and the goal grabbing of Jimmy McLaughlin, the free scoring Town left winger, are both fundamental reasons for Rotherham's slender lead. Whatever the outcome of this double-barrelled battle, however, the fact remains that the initial phase, on the Millmoor front, will be remembered as an outstanding game of the season. In my opinion, it stands out as the most thrilling and the most entertaining match of the season so far at Rotherham. A different brand of football entirely from that of the dismal affair at Luton last weekend. Before the match the fire brigade watered the pitch. Thus, the threat of scrappy dry ground soccer was eliminated. One of the most pleasing and heartening features of the game, from the Rotherham angle, was the display of something like his best form by Brian Sawyer. He gave United vigorous, enthusiastic, and strong striking leadership. He scored two goals – his first in the League Cup – and with any luck might have had double that number. And his speed and accurate distribution created more chances for his colleagues. Often, and justifiably so, the forward line gets the brickbats and the defence gets the bouquets. Sure the forwards could, and should, have hit more goals – Kirkman was particularly erratic – but in my view, the United defence slipped up badly in allowing Shrewsbury to score at all. The defence was confused and Ironside was out of position when the first goal came and half backs and full backs were at sixes and sevens when the second was scored. Personally, I cannot understand why some of the crowd singled out Kirkman for such severe verbal treatment. Certainly, he merits criticism for his wild finishing and for that especially bad early miss, but let us give him his due share of credit for enterprising football. He is United's best outside right even if he does need to steady his shooting. Both the United inside forwards disappointed me. Weston, despite his great centre for the opening goal, is capable of much more positive work, and Houghton must make more contribution to the team effort, constructive and skilful as his ball distribution often is. Bambridge did some very fine work indeed, in his best tricky, incisive style, and he received some rough handling from the Shrewsbury defence when his elusiveness got the men in blue desperately worried.

Inexplicably, he was neglected at times in the second half and the crowd cheered ironically when he was given the ball. I admired the exquisite distribution of Waterhouse in the first half, flashes of the finest football of Madden and Morgan, and the vital and high grade second half saves of Ironside, but the United defence frequently lacked all round solidity and conceded their first goals in the League Cup since they played at Leicester last October. It was in fact, the first time that Rotherham had yielded more than a single goal in a single game in this competition. Lambert had a poor game and Perry was unimpressive. United were ahead in six minutes. Weston put over a perfect deep centre from the right wing and Sawyer headed the ball down and into the net from point blank range, by the far post, for his first League Cup goal. After eleven minutes, United should have been two up. Sawyer provided some momentarily inspired football to burst his way through on the left wing and crossed a low pass to the feet of Kirkman standing inside the six yard area. But Kirkman spooned the ball high over the crossbar. Perry checked McLaughlin with a first class tackle and a shot from Arthur Rowley curled narrowly past the United woodwork. Then we were treated to a glimpse of the Bambridge magic and he put over an extremely dangerous centre, which two United forwards in the middle failed to make use of. Rotherham could have been three goals up in the first quarter of an hour, but they got a second in the eighteenth minute. Houghton centred the ball from the left, and a brief, but hectic, scramble round the Shrewsbury goal finished with Sawyer slashing the ball home from short range. Up to this stage, Ironside had not had a ball to save, but he was fishing the ball from the back of the net a minute later. A header from Rowley laid on the shock goal chance for McLaughlin, the scoring winger with the instinct for being in the right place at the crucial moment. With Ironside out of position and the whole United defence disarranged, the winger, scorer of twenty-three goals this season, nodded the ball home. It was the first League Cup goal against Rotherham at Millmoor. For an exciting spell, we saw the best of Sawyer, who was robbed of a 'hat trick' by the brilliant goalkeeping of Gibson. First Gibson had to dive to keep out a powerful shot, then he made flying saves from two Sawyer headers, both from Kirkman centres. Another Sawyer shot sizzled inches wide and Morgan sent in a hard left foot drive which Gibson plucked out of the air in spectacular style. The interval came after Kirkman had blazed the ball over the bar from a Houghton pass. On the resumption, Shrewsbury attacked in telling fashion, and Ironside made splendid saves from Baker, McLaughlin and Rowley. But United restored their two goal lead after only nine minutes in the second half. Bambridge dribbled into the middle, beating Corbett, who then vainly followed him, and chipped the ball cleverly into the penalty area. Kirkman was on the spot for the pass and the ball rolled into the net off his chest as Gibson and Pountney harassed him. Shrewsbury narrowed the goals gap again, however, with eleven minutes to go. Jones, a short winger with a Bambridge look, dribbled unchallenged down the centre of United territory and finally slipped the ball through to the unmarked McLaughlin, who crashed it past the helpless Ironside. Shrewsbury must have been satisfied with the result. In the early stages, they looked as though they were in for a thrashing, but they did not get one. One thing is certain, I am looking forward to the match at Shrewsbury with relish. It should be a thriller. United: Ironside; Perry, Morgan; Lambert, Madden, Waterhouse; Kirkman, Weston, Sawyer, Houghton, Bambridge. Shrewsbury: Gibson; Corbett, Walters; Wallace, Pountney, Harley; Jones, Starkey, Baker, Rowley, McLaughlin. Referee: Mr J.G. Williams (Nottingham)."

John Piper meanwhile, reporting in the *Sheffield Star* dated Wednesday 22nd March 1961, filed a strange and eccentric report, in which he completely forgot to mention Rotherham United's first two goals! His missive noted: "Once upon a time there was a comedy film strip called The Perils of Pauline – full of incredible absurdities with broad humour. And in places of the first semi final of the Football League Cup at Millmoor it was almost as if United's leading marksman, Alan Kirkman, was trying to play the role! This is the man whose greatest soccer asset, at least at Rotherham, has been his chance and half-chance taking. Poor fellow. He could do no right to start with. He – though not alone – should have packed Shrewsbury's hopes into an old tin trunk within twenty minutes of the kick off. Some misses were fantastic. Yet somehow Kirkman, with just the right knack, always contrives to be there at the right minute. Having jettisoned so much, he very pluckily got the third goal as three Town defenders tried to crush him. That should have put United at 3-1 on an easy ride, but the game was allowed to bog down for a time. Shrewsbury, wonderfully served by the blonde lawful fury of centre half Dave Pountney, sensed there was still a chance to cut the score line. McLaughlin who scored the first, did the job after good preparation by opposite winger Jones – who is two inches shorter than Bambridge. There was not much danger after this, and Shrewsbury finished in comfort. Rotherham's backward glance at this game should be one of satisfaction that it contained good entertainment (in one way and another) and sharp self criticism at the many discarded chances of having won in wide comfort. I still consider they will win through to the final providing such dreadful waste of goal chances is not repeated." In the *Rotherham Advertiser* dated 25th March 1961 'Echo' commented: "United go to Gay Meadow only one goal up, but that need not be regarded as a fatal disadvantage, despite the fact that the vociferous zeal of the capacity partisan Shrewsbury crowd will back up Town's team effort to the hilt. After all, if this tie was a straightforward one-match tussle, with United drawn away, they would be starting on level terms, not with a goal in hand. United have only themselves to blame, regardless of Shrewsbury's never-say-die spirit at Millmoor, for not going into the return game with a lead of several goals and let us not be unduly lugubrious about their prospects." When asked about this match on 25th February 2005, Brian Sawyer was quite modest about his goal scoring achievements, merely commenting: "We really expected to beat Shrewsbury, even though they had just knocked out Everton. I can't remember being particularly excited after the match – just satisfied."

The Millers therefore came out of the first leg game without the three goal cushion that the programme editor thought was necessary to guarantee reaching the final. The crucial second leg was played at Shrewsbury Town's Gay Meadow ground on Wednesday 29th March 1961 with everything to play for, and the tie delicately poised. It could not have been tighter until, in extra time, a Don Weston goal secured Rotherham United a 1-1 draw to send them through to the Final with a 4-3 aggregate victory.

The Shrewsbury Town match programme (at price 6d double the cost of the United issue) noted: "A special welcome is extended to Rotherham United tonight with thanks to them for the hospitality, kindness and sportsmanship shown to our team, officials and supporters at last Tuesday's game. ... Many people, Press and Clubs, had decided before the Cup Competition had even begun that it was a dead loss. We at Shrewsbury do not subscribe to that view and as always confirm our loyalty to our Parent Body and support the tourney to the hilt. Whilst we do not deny that success in the competition has

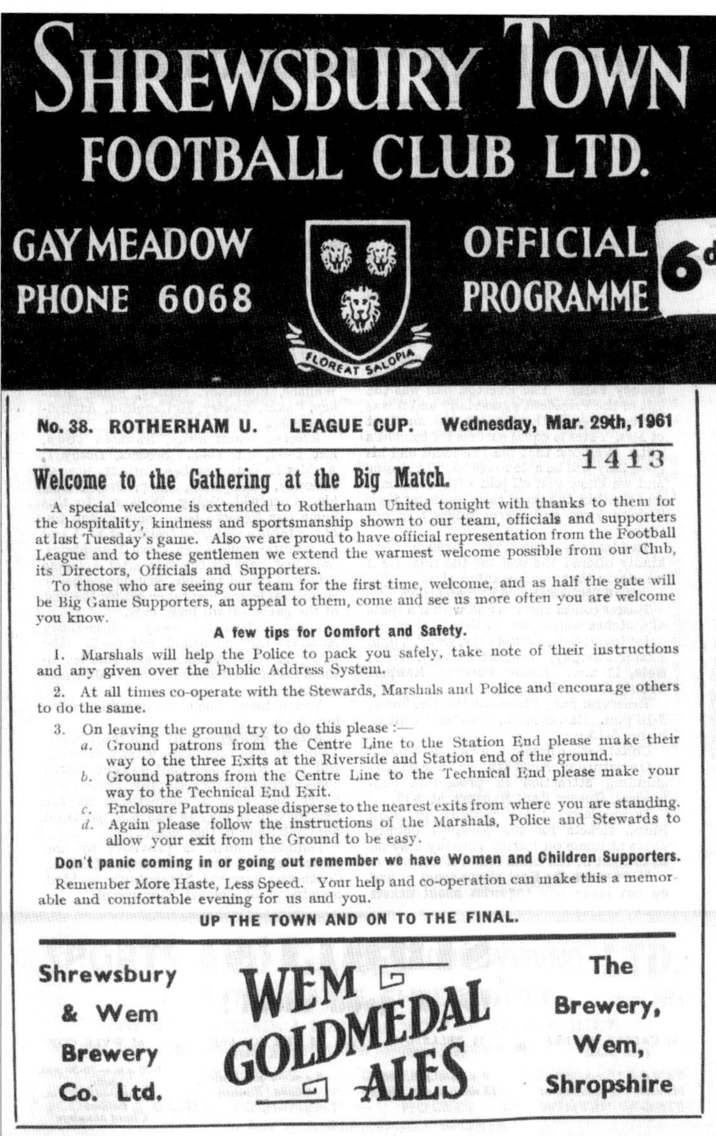

SHREWSBURY TOWN
FOOTBALL CLUB LTD.
GAY MEADOW
PHONE 6068
OFFICIAL
PROGRAMME
6d.
FLOREAT SALOPIA

No. 38. ROTHERHAM U. LEAGUE CUP. Wednesday, Mar. 29th, 1961

1413

Welcome to the Gathering at the Big Match.

A special welcome is extended to Rotherham United tonight with thanks to them for the hospitality, kindness and sportsmanship shown to our team, officials and supporters at last Tuesday's game. Also we are proud to have official representation from the Football League and to these gentlemen we extend the warmest welcome possible from our Club, its Directors, Officials and Supporters.

To those who are seeing our team for the first time, welcome, and as half the gate will be Big Game Supporters, an appeal to them, come and see us more often you are welcome you know.

A few tips for Comfort and Safety.

1. Marshals will help the Police to pack you safely, take note of their instructions and any given over the Public Address System.

2. At all times co-operate with the Stewards, Marshals and Police and encourage others to do the same.

3. On leaving the ground try to do this please :—
   a. Ground patrons from the Centre Line to the Station End please make their way to the three Exits at the Riverside and Station end of the ground.
   b. Ground patrons from the Centre Line to the Technical End please make your way to the Technical End Exit.
   c. Enclosure Patrons please disperse to the nearest exits from where you are standing.
   d. Again please follow the instructions of the Marshals, Police and Stewards to allow your exit from the Ground to be easy.

Don't panic coming in or going out remember we have Women and Children Supporters.

Remember More Haste, Less Speed. Your help and co-operation can make this a memorable and comfortable evening for us and you.

UP THE TOWN AND ON TO THE FINAL.

Shrewsbury & Wem Brewery Co. Ltd.
WEM GOLDMEDAL ALES
The Brewery, Wem, Shropshire

Shrewsbury Town versus Rotherham United programme, for the hard-fought second leg of the semi final on Wednesday 29th March 1961. (Graham Barnes collection)

brought financial reward to Players and Club alike, we must not let the imagination run rife and think that vast sums of £ s. d. have been made, but we do say that what has been made has been very useful and a welcome addition to club coffers." Accounts were published showing total receipts, for Shrewsbury Town's run to the semi final second leg, as £2,028 17s 6d, with a net profit of £533 18s 0d.

The *Rotherham Advertiser* dated Saturday 1st April 1961 reported that: "It was appropriate that Don Weston should score the goal that sent Rotherham United into the first ever League Cup final when the semi-final second leg was played at Shrewsbury on Wednesday. The result was a 1-1 draw and United won 4-3 on goals aggregate after 3½ hours play. Before he equalised straight from the restart after the second interval of the match, Weston almost made extra time unnecessary twice in the last three minutes of normal time. In the 87th minute, Sawyer put the ball through the middle. There was a chase between Weston and Mike Gibson the Shrewsbury goalkeeper. Weston won the race for the ball and shot narrowly wide. Then, in the last minute, Weston volleyed the ball hard with his left foot. And the ball crashed against the upright, with Gibson flat out in a despairing dive and obviously beaten. If either of those drives had been a shade nearer the mark, the Rotherham team and their supporters would have been able to set off home half an hour sooner. Shrewsbury, starting 3-2 down, brought the aggregate to 3-3 after fifteen minutes with a totally unexpected 'gift' goal, greeted with thunderous cheers by the 16,722 crowd. The goal was a personal tragedy for Peter Madden, but it was not his fault. Wiley Arthur Rowley attempted a through pass, but Madden appeared to have the ball covered and no danger to United was even remotely suspected. Madden slipped, however, on the greasy surface – the fire brigade had been in action at Gay Meadow as well as Millmoor – and inside right Starkey was able to fasten easily on to the ball and go on to drive in past Roy Ironside. The goalkeeper himself had been placed in a hopeless position. For the following 105 minutes it was sheer slogging all the way for both sides in a battle that was a stern test of stamina. Defenders prepared to yield absolutely nothing repulsed attack after attack, but there were some narrow escapes for hosts and guests alike notwithstanding. After falling behind, United were uneasy for a short time, but every man in the rearguard put all he had in the way of determination and endeavour into a combined effort to stop the darting raids of the Shrewsbury forwards. And the United forwards worked hard in midfield in a concerted attempt to break down the Town defensive barrier, a barrier which took a lot of demolishing. Eventually, however, United emerged triumphant and finished their long, hard stint with an air of dominant composure. Ironside made some fine saves in an assured goalkeeping display and the full backs, Peter Perry and Lol Morgan, fought like terriers. All the half backs touched peak form, tackling and chasing hard, and covering up well. Madden towered in the centre after his unlucky involuntary slip, and Roy Lambert and Ken Waterhouse performed heroically at wing half. Waterhouse played superbly and a feature of the match was his intelligent and constructive use of the ball to switch defence into attack. It was heartening from a Rotherham angle to see Weston producing something like his best form again. There was a lot of his characteristic dash and thrust and clear evidence of his hard hitting style of marksmanship. With any luck, he would have had a hat trick. Brian Sawyer, United hero of the first leg, had an interesting tussle with Dave Pountney, Shrewsbury's excellent centre half, and although he did not make such a telling impact on this game in terms of goals and finishing power, he laid on some fine shooting chances for his colleagues. Alan Kirkman, playing at inside left, had a quiet, but useful role. Barry Webster worked hard and Keith Bambridge frequently harassed the Shrewsbury defence with his trickery. Bambridge in fact, almost gave United an early lead and he was only thwarted by the brilliant goalkeeping of Gibson. After the Shrewsbury goal, George Baker, whose deep lying centre forward role was largely negative, put in a drive which curled just outside the Rotherham woodwork and fleet footed Jimmy McLaughlin, scorer of two goals at Millmoor, was given offside after hitting the bar. Town played the better football for a time after taking the lead, but when United hit back, Gibson had to be agile to prevent an equaliser on several occasions and there were some narrow escapes during scrambles round their goal. Three minutes before the break, Weston went close with a drive which cleared the crossbar by inches. On the resumption, both sides tried desperately to get the ball past the men in the green sweaters. United had a break when McLaughlin slammed the ball against the bar and Ironside whipped the rebound from Harley's toes. Madden cleared off the goal line and Lambert then prevented what must have been a certain goal if he had not covered up so quickly. After a brilliant dribble, McLaughlin did everything but put the ball on a plate for Rowley, but the United captain covered up swiftly to block the Shrewsbury skipper's drive. Close calls, indeed, for United, but Shrewsbury were lucky twice in three minutes. Put through by Sawyer and left with an almost clear run through the middle, Weston was off the mark quick as a flash and beat Gibson to the ball. The goalkeeper finished on his knees and Weston fired the ball narrowly wide of an empty goal. A miss it certainly was, but it was a bit of good luck for Shrewsbury. Two minutes later, Weston's brilliant volley – the shot of the match – shook an upright. The struggle continued for another fifteen minutes, but Weston sent United into the Final in the first minute of the second half of extra time. United attacked from the kick off and Weston took Sawyer's pass from the right and scored with a shot that sent the ball bouncing into the net via Gibson's body. Sawyer laid on another chance for Weston, but he skied the ball wide and United might have scored again on another occasion if Weston had passed the ball to unmarked team mates in good shooting positions. Shrewsbury: Gibson; Walters, Skeech; Wallace, Pountney, Harley; Jones, Starkey, Baker, Rowley, McLaughlin. United: Ironside; Perry, Morgan; Lambert, Madden, Waterhouse; Webster, Weston, Sawyer, Kirkman, Bambridge. Referee: Mr N.N. Hough (Macclesfield)."

The *Sheffield Star* dated Thursday 30th March 1961 reported: "So it is a cup final for Rotherham after all, but the last stage at Shrewsbury was not without its patches of torture and long spells under the spur of warm-hearted and good footballing opposition. In the end the result was right for United's place in the first final of the Football League Cup against either Villa or Burnley. They got away to a brilliant, relaxed standard that showed Town up as an infinitely poorer outfit. Then came the man-made mud-patch – good intentioned flooding by the fire brigade – which rocked Madden on his back and let in the ex-Blackpool man Starkey for a 16th minute goal. That put the situation all square and the long haul began for United. At half time you might have laid Shrewsbury 6-4 prospective winners, but by failing to press home their advantage when Rotherham's pulse was jerky and weakest, Shrewsbury found themselves slowly but surely heading for failure. Failure that is to beat down a defence that got more and more organised. More and more it became clear that only an accident was going to beat the Yorkshire men. Peter Perry put an increasingly tight straight jacket on the slippery sharp-shooting McLaughlin who

Rotherham United's principal twelve players who fought their way to the first ever League Cup final. Lining up on the back row are six defenders, left to right: Roy Lambert, Ken Waterhouse, Peter Madden, Roy Ironside, Lol Morgan and Peter Perry. The six forwards on the front row are, left to right: Brian Sawyer, Barry Webster, Don Weston, Ken Houghton, Alan Kirkman and Keith Bambridge. (Rotherham United)

twice hit the bar. The wing half backs and the supreme Madden had sorted out the puzzle of the opposition's deep-lying centre forward. Morgan, as neat and unruffled as a tailor's dummy, cut out all the right flank threat. Up front United had their own semi-deep attack leader now. Sawyer, moved to the wing in the face of Pountney's command when the line was orthodox, began to stride out. Webster chased around on a loose commission leaving Weston and Kirkman to be twin-triggers. Indeed it was the Weston-Sawyer link that provided the equaliser in the 106th minute. Weston had already beaten a fearless Gibson with a rocket drive that flashed back off the post. The goal that mattered was well executed. The formation that produced it could leave manager Tom Johnston thinking on such lines for his perilous League Two Easter parade. Overall the blind-buff passages did not matter. It was good entertainment, a credit in every respect to Shrewsbury, a side for whom 'Boss' Rowley frequently gave elementary lessons in how defences should be beaten by a skilfully-used ball. His indignity was the late penalty hopeful dive that just looked like a learner swimmer risking a small wave at low tide. As things worked out, Keith Bambridge has not to wear a mourning wreath over three, possibly four, scoring chances that were brother to those of Alan Kirkman in the first tie. Those golden faces with the super-fund of scoring opportunity simply must not be dumped time and again if Rotherham are to do justice to themselves."

Speaking on 14th May 2005, Brian Sawyer recalled the away leg at Shrewsbury Town: "One of our Directors owned Smart's Coaches, and we travelled to the game on the day of the match by coach. [Cyril Smart was the Director to whom Brian refers, and the garage was opposite the 'new baths' on Sheffield Road.] We always had a hard core of away supporters, and there was a band of Millers fans at the game. It was all very different in those days, however, and at the end of the game there was none of the modern-style mutual admiration applauding each other. Even though we had just won our way through to the cup final, we just walked off the field at the whistle. It was very low key. We came back in the coach and arrived in Rotherham in the early hours, with some of the players getting dropped off near their homes. Lol Morgan was the first Rotherham United player to own his own car, a VW 'Beetle', and he gave a couple of players a lift. Somehow we all got home to our beds!"

The Millers had won through by the narrowest of margins, and the Final would be contested by First Division Aston Villa and Second Division Rotherham United. It is interesting to compare how the two clubs made it through. Aston Villa took the long road, having to play no less than ten matches, including replays, and had an overall goal difference of 26 for and 15 against. Rotherham United did it the easy way, conceding only one goal prior to the semi-final, and cruising to the final in the minimum possible six matches, achieving a goal difference of 13 for and only 4 against. Besides the fabulous achievement of reaching the final, and the publicity it brought to the township of Rotherham, the cup run also had a lesser known benefit – in the form of monetary reward for the players. Ken Houghton recalls that: "a payment structure had been negotiated before the tournament began whereby the club would pay the players an ever-increasing bonus if and when progress was achieved through each round. As things turned out the squad made good money for that era, with the League Cup paying us big bonuses!" [see the later newspaper report, confirming Rotherham United were on over £100 a man.] Mavis Lambert (Roy's wife) recalled on 10th June 2005 that: "As I remember it, there was a £4 bonus for winning in the second round at Leicester, then £8 for the third round, and doubling each round up to the final. So presumably there was a £64 bonus by the time Shewsbury were beaten in the semi-final, and they would have been on £128 if they had won the final."

By the time Aston Villa had won their semi-final decider on 2nd May 1961, the 1960/61 season was all but over. The more glamorous F.A. Cup Final was to be held only four days later, when Leicester City were to meet Tottenham Hotspur at Wembley. Leicester City (who, of course, had been knocked out of the League Cup by Rotherham United) lost the Wembley showdown 0-2. There simply was no time to fit in the League Cup Final as well, and its management committee made the only decision that was feasible, and held over the 1960/61 final to the beginning of the 1961/62 season.

In summer 1961, in the close season between the semi final and final of the League Cup, the Millers undertook a tour of Finland. This rare photograph shows the game played in the Olympic Stadium, Helsinki, with Peter Perry about to play the ball (left), Peter Madden (number 5, centre) and Roy Lambert running to cover (right). (Peter Perry collection)

With the 1960/61 season out of the way, Rotherham United set out on a close season tour of Finland. Speaking in January 2005, Ken Houghton recalled: "The club arranged a coach for us, and we set off from Millmoor and headed off down to Tilbury Docks. We then set out on a 48 hour sailing in rough seas, with the ship tossed about in the waves, and only about two or three of the entire party were not seasick. Everybody looked very green when we disembarked at Gothenburg!" Peter Perry recalls that one of their matches was played in the Olympic Stadium in Helsinki, and also that during the tour the team had a guided tour around a timber plant. During another official visit every player was presented with an unusual gift, namely a metal cooking pot! [Peter's still resides in their kitchen cupboard, and it was shown to the author!] Keith Bambridge remembers the tour well and said: "I was one of the fortunate people who was not seasick, but it was a terrible crossing. It was my own first time abroad. We played about four friendly matches, including a 4-0 win against Aliance, the Finland League representative side. They were not a strong team, but they had an important game coming up against then champions of Brazil, Vasco da Gama FC, who were also touring. As a result, Tom Johnston was asked if three Rotherham United players could be released to strengthen the Aliance side, and he agreed to release myself, Don Weston and Ken Houghton. No caps or medals were awarded, but Aliance won the match 1-0." It is therefore interesting, and perhaps a little known fact, that Rotherham United has three former players with Finland representative honours!

5. The First ever Final

It was the beginning of season 1961/62, therefore, that witnessed the two-legs of the first ever (1960/61) Football League Cup Final. On Tuesday 22nd August 1961, a crowd of 12,226 assembled at Millmoor for the historic first leg against Aston Villa, a club that was a founder member (1888) of the Football League. Aston Villa had proved to be hardy cup fighters over many years and history showed that they had appeared in the F.A. Cup final on nine occasions, 1887-92-95-97, 1905-13-20-24-57, and won seven of them. A ticket in the stand for the final cost 7s 6d (37p). Writing in the Rotherham United match programme (price 3d) for the final, the editor bemoaned the failure to complete the event in the previous season and commented: "That in no way detracts from the welcome we extend to one of the game's great clubs – Aston Villa – all the more welcome because they come under the charge of one of the nicest guys in the business, Joe Mercer. It is just that, at the end of last term, everyone hereabouts was keyed up, eager for the two-match decision of the final. The interest had been built and bolstered by the succession of victories, two of them against first division opponents away from home. The mood was just right for a final tie. With the best will in the world, and while the attraction as always of the Villa remains, the setting tonight has not the same appeal. Just the same we look for a capital game both here and at Birmingham on September 5th." The editor went on to mention that Aston Villa would be: "without Gerry Hitchens of course, who is seeking his football fortune in the land of the lira". England international centre forward Gerry Hitchens had been a goal scorer for Aston Villa in the club's 1960/61 League Cup run, and he was an articulate player with finesse. Gerry had been transferred to Italian giants Internazionale of Milan in the close season and, although Millers supporters would miss out on watching a great player, perhaps they thought it would give Rotherham a better chance of victory.

The final was a poignant occasion for Brian Sawyer, who had played in five of the six games leading up to the final, but did not appear in the big showdown. When asked about this in February 2005 Brian said: "I had played in all bar one of the previous rounds, and helped us win away at First Division clubs Leicester City and Bolton Wanderers, and I scored twice in the first leg of the semi final against Shrewsbury. Indeed, I think the game away at Bolton was the best we played while I was at Rotherham, and even better than those Arsenal games. However, the final was delayed until the following season and it was on our close season tour in Finland that I injured my knee. It was operated on in July 1961 and I was not ready in time for the final. After that my knee was not really strong enough for playing at maximum effort in the professional game, although when I dropped into the non-league scene I could hide it. I still have the scars to this day."

In a nail biting match, the final was goal-less at half time. In the second period, Barry Webster despatched the ball into the Aston Villa net to go down in history as the scorer of the first ever goal in a League Cup Final. Alan Kirkman scored a second for Rotherham United, whilst a great penalty save by Roy Ironside preserved the Millers' advantage. The *Rotherham*

How times have changed! A cup final ticket, in a reserved seat, Row B, seat number 5, at a cost of just 7s 6d (37p). This ticket is diagonally over-stamped 'Complimentary'. (Adrian Booth collection)

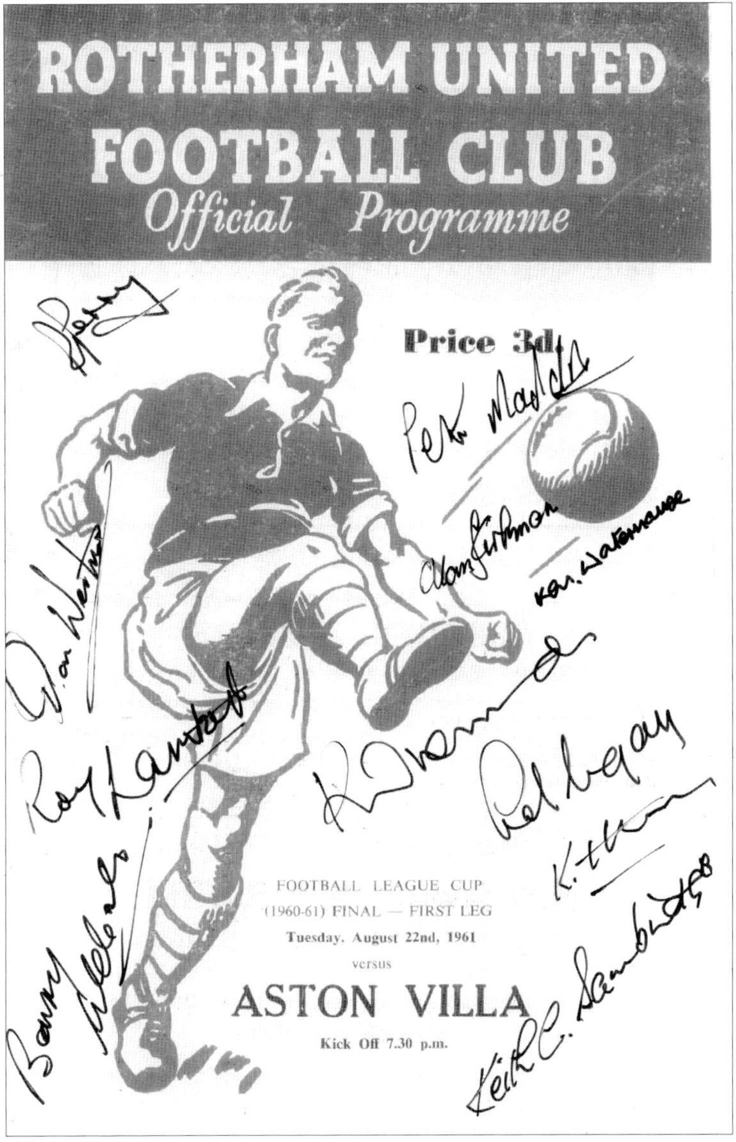

The author's copy of the League Cup Final first leg programme, for the match played on Tuesday 22nd August 1961. During the period December 2004 to April 2005, it was autographed by all eleven players who played in that historic occasion. On the left side (top to bottom) it is signed by Peter Perry, Don Weston, Roy Lambert and Barry Webster. On the right side (top to bottom) the signatures are Peter Madden, Alan Kirkman, Ken Waterhouse, Roy Ironside, Lol Morgan, Ken Houghton and Keith Bambridge. (Adrian Booth)

Advertiser dated Saturday 26th August 1961 reported: "If the Football League Cup, in its second season, can produce thrilling and powerful football anything like that which characterised the 'left-over' final of its first season, then the future of the new competition is assured. Moreover the five First Division clubs now standing aloof from the competition might have second thoughts if we are to see in this season's Football League Cup crowd-pulling football of the sort Rotherham United and Aston Villa produced at Millmoor on Tuesday evening. For Rotherham it was a night of triumph. They won 2-0, thanks to a great display in the second half, and they must now fancy their chances of becoming the first winners of the League Cup. A hard task lies ahead of them, of course, in the second leg of the final at Villa Park next month. Their First Division opponents make tough opposition on their own ground, as Rotherham found to their cost when they last visited the Aston enclosure in a League match, but the Villa were then on the verge of ascending into the higher class of football and they had the celebrated Hitchens at centre forward. Now he has departed to sunnier climes, and Villa can't play the dashing Derek Dougan (ex Blackburn Rovers) in the middle because he is not eligible for the 1960/61 competition. On Tuesday they had a seventeen year old player, Ralph Brown, in his place, and although he showed distinct promise he lacks the experience needed for such encounters as Tuesday night's, as was evidenced by the number of times he stopped Villa movements by getting himself involved in unnecessary fouls. There are plenty of Rotherham followers who in spite of the United's well-deserved success on Tuesday, are inclined to pessimism about the ultimate outcome of this clash between Yorkshire and the Midlands.

Without minimising Rotherham's task against this robust Villa side, it is comforting to point to the two goals advantage Rotherham enjoy. If they keep their heads at Villa Park they have a wonderful chance of bringing to Millmoor the highest national distinction ever achieved by the club. Come to think of it, they have already brought such distinction with their performance in the first leg.

A newspaper cutting showing Alan Kirkman being beaten to the ball by Aston Villa goalkeeper Nigel Sims, in the first leg of the final at Millmoor. (Graham Barnes collection)

And now to Tuesday's game. It turned out to be a reversal of the United tendency to get on top and then falter – a tendency observed as recently as last Saturday at Stoke. On Tuesday they kept the really powerful stuff until the early minutes of the second half, when they punched home two fine goals. To administer a double blow from which Villa (who had earlier looked capable of winning at their ease) never recovered. The first after 52 minutes might well be called a 'W-plan' affair for it was a defence splitting pass by Weston that led to Webster crashing the ball past Nigel Sims, in the Villa goal. Weston's perfect pass enabled Houghton to head the ball through for Webster to run in and, taking his chance first time, leave Sims helpless. Weston will never achieve better football artistry than that move. A further triumph was to come within three minutes. Bambridge, who up to that point had not been having a particularly distinguished game – he had been at the receiving end of some over-robust defensive work – held on to the ball admirably when challenged near goal, and provided Kirkman with the chance to head home Rotherham's second with Sims lured out of goal. Within minutes Rotherham hearts stood still as Villa were awarded a penalty kick for a foul judged to have been committed by Lambert. It was, in the opinion of most Rotherham followers, a harsh decision. But there it was, and up strode the Villa full back Stan Lynn, to take the kick. It was a powerful enough shot, but Roy Ironside went down to the ball with all the assurance of a goalkeeper in form (he had dramatically demonstrated that in saving a terrific shot from Thomson in the first half), and Rotherham were saved the necessity of going to Birmingham with an advantage of only one goal. Rotherham might have had a chance, soon afterwards, of showing that they have a more reliable penalty kick marksman in Perry, for Bambridge was sent flying in the 'box', but the referee's decision went against them. So much for that pulsating second half. Of the first half it can be said that Villa carried the greater punch. Their passing was more accurate than Rotherham's, and in MacEwan they had a winger who always looked capable of winning the match off his own bat; unfortunately for Villa it was just as evident that, on Tuesday's showing, McParland is no longer the power that he was. For a time in the second half he took over from young Brown at centre forward but produced no fireworks of the old McParland kind. Rotherham's was a triumph of team work. It could not be said that any one player was more outstanding than another, but they coasted to victory against their First Division opponents by the punch they found in the second half. Darlington, Rotherham's opponents in the first round of the 1961/62 competition (the match to be played at Darlington) will consider, on this showing, that they have something on their plate. Teams: Rotherham United: Ironside; Perry, Morgan; Lambert, Madden, Waterhouse; Webster, Weston, Houghton, Kirkman, Bambridge. Aston Villa: Sims; Lynn, Lee; Crowe, Dugdale, Deakin; MacEwan, Thomson, Brown, Wylie, McParland."

In a separate item the *Rotherham Advertiser* dated 26th August 1961 reported: "The attendance at Millmoor for the Aston Villa game – 12,226 – was a disappointment, especially in view of Rotherham's success at Stoke [a 2-1 victory] last Saturday. The relatively low 'gate' for a League Cup final may well have been part of the penalty to be paid for holding over the 1960/61 game to the new season. Had the match been played last season – as it could have been had Aston Villa and Burnley settled the semi final issue more expeditiously – the attendance at Millmoor would certainly have exceeded 12,226. As it is, there has scarcely been time for supporters on both sides to have their interest brought to 'Cup Final' pitch." In a further tit-bit the newspaper noted: "The penalty incident at Millmoor on Tuesday night was the second episode of the Ironside-Lynn penalty story. When the teams last met on 23rd April 1960 [Aston Villa won 3-0] Villa were awarded a spot kick, which was taken by Lynn. As on Monday, the Rotherham goalkeeper stopped the Villa full-back's shot, but on that occasion he could not do any more than push the ball out, and Thomson, following up, managed to score."

Meanwhile, in the *Sheffield Star* dated Wednesday 23rd August 1961, John Piper reported: "You could do worse than begin the tale of Rotherham's success in Match One of the first Football League Cup Final at the unobvious end. For United, complete winners, have to praise keeper Ironside for key-point saves: in 18 minutes when he stopped Thomson opening the score with as astonishing a save as we shall see all the year, and again for second half saving of the Lynn penalty. Stan Lynn, one of the mightiest dead ball kickers in the business, took his kick at a critical time for Rotherham. From there on, as indeed before in the late first half, Rotherham cut or rolled their way to supremacy against a Villa side that hurried and scurried. Hardly ever did the Villa half backs establish a counter to the double stabbing done by Kirkman and Weston. Finally there was no question about the right of Rotherham to go to Villa Park on September 5, two goals up. Said Joe Mercer: "Rotherham thoroughly deserved to win." Said Tom Johnston: "Very satisfactory. We did extremely well once we had got over the first quarter of an hour or so." Throw away by all means most of the first half. Like all the other Villa-Rotherham matches, those taking part were jittery and prone to error. One exception was Peter Madden, hungry not only for his own duty but to help any colleagues in difficulty. Seventeen year old Ralph Brown had little chance but stuck to it and showed enough to make one sigh for a blueprint in the Millmoor nursery. Individual skill lies in this Villa team. Their teamwork was, this night, not in the same bracket as United's. And more than anything the home side mocked their opponents with their sweet linkage between half backs and forwards. First goal by Barry Webster was a stunner. He began it 30 yards inside his own half and, helped first by Weston, then Houghton (another good match) he finished it with all the happy memory style of his regular goal getting days. Let's hope that this new campaign, with time healing Webster's personal sorrow of last term, is to be bright for him. Little Keith Bambridge, who gave us light relief early in the game when he and the huge Lynn 'fell out', trussed up the Villa defence entirely for Kirkman to head the second goal. I went on record expecting Rotherham to win this match. A fortnight hence they may not repeat the result but their two goal advantage will, to their infinite credit, probably put the League Cup in the Millmoor boardroom at the first time of award." At least John Piper had every confidence that Rotherham United would win the cup!

Another match report from the collection of Graham Barnes (newspaper unidentified) recorded: "The night was young when Aston Villa inside-right Bobby Thomson shot the perfect

***Below.* An action shot from the final first leg, with Alan Kirkman sprawling on the ground after powering a header just wide of the post. Seven Aston Villa players, including goalkeeper Nigel Sims, look on anxiously. (Adrian Booth collection)**

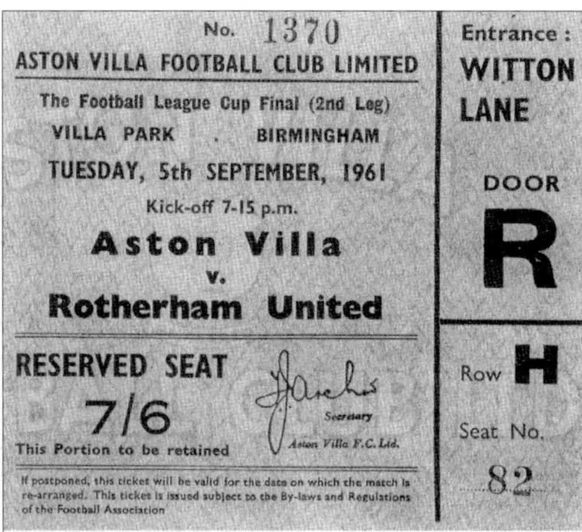

Match ticket for the second leg of the final on 5th September 1961. A seat in the stand cost 7s 6d, the same price as the match at Millmoor. (Graham Barnes collection)

volley from eight yards in the first leg of the big-money League Cup final at Rotherham last night. The ball had staked its own corner of the net until Roy Ironside, that United goalkeeper of the amazing reflexes, dived to his left to make the most incredible save I have seen in three matches this season and over 60 last term. Ralph Brown, Villa's 17 year old debutant leader from Ilkeston, Derbyshire – deputising for the ineligible Derek Dougan – looked on as if to say: 'If that can't get a goal, what can?' This was destined to be Ironside's night. The League Cup winners can pick up over £100 a man. If Rotherham win it after the second leg on September 5, Ironside will have deserved no less. For over half an hour from that 17th minute, neither forward line seemed to have the confidence or ability to score against expert defences – and then suddenly Rotherham became United again. They played chess-soccer at ice-hockey pace. From deep in his own half, right winger Barry Webster started the move. He passed to Don Weston, who passed to Ken Houghton, who passed it back to Webster. From the inside right position and a bad angle, he lofted the ball over Nigel Sims's right shoulder for goal number one. Four minutes later Keith Bambridge pulled back the ball from the left by-line and Alan Kirkman headed number two. I had not given Rotherham a chance of breaking down this Villa back door and Joe Mercer's men were equally astonished when they were two down. When Peter McParland finally emerged as a dangerous marksman for the first time with a typical drive from 18 yards, the goalkeeper amazingly got a fingertip – I'm sure it was only one – to divert the ball. In the 73rd minute, Roy Lambert forgot his previous good manners and tripped Thomson in the penalty box. Stan Lynn's spot kick was too straight and the over-stretching body of Ironside blocked the ball on the line. Young Brown had a tough night against Rotherham pivot Peter Madden – nearly as tough as the whole Villa team had against Ironside, who made three important saves – how vital they were!"

Speaking at his home in Hull on 5th May 2005, Ken Houghton recalled nodding the ball through for Barry Webster to score the first goal and smiled: "Barry was so pleased to have scored that he set off running round the pitch in celebration. The rest of us tried to catch him, but we had to run round practically the whole pitch. When we finally caught him we were all knackered!" Barry laughed when told (at his home in Sheffield on 9th June 2005) about Ken's story and responded: "Yes, it's true I set off running round the pitch. I had experienced some very sad times in my personal life around that time, leading to a loss of form on the pitch, and when my shot hit the back of the net it was a sort of release for me. How it happened was that Roy Ironside threw the ball out to me, in our own half, and I passed it on to Don Weston and then ran off down the right wing. Meanwhile, Don cleverly picked out Ken Houghton, who saw me arriving and headed the ball nicely into my path. By this time I was on the corner of the penalty box and hit a shot that went high into the net, beating Nigel Sims on the near post. I don't really know how it went in from that angle."

At his home in Bramley on 15th April 2005, Keith Bambridge could vividly remember setting up Rotherham's second goal: "I was put through on the left side of Villa's box and saw their goalkeeper Nigel Sims come diving out, spreading his body towards my feet. In these circumstances, things flash through your brain in a split second and I thought that if I shot for goal the ball would be blocked by Sims. I managed to lift the ball over the keeper and chip it towards the far post. Alan Kirkman was a really excellent header of the ball, and was one of those players who had that uncanny ability to hover in the air. Alan was there towards the back post and headed home from just underneath the crossbar." When talking about this goal with Brian Sawyer on 14th May 2005, he agreed with Keith's assessment, recalling: "Alan Kirkman was exceptionally good in the air".

On 9th June 2005 Roy Ironside was asked about his penalty save. He modestly commented: "To be honest I cannot particularly remember much about it. During my many years playing in goal I faced lots of penalty kicks and it is difficult now to remember one in particular. When I was out on the pitch and about to face a penalty kick, I used to closely watch the taker to see if I could pick up any clues as to where he was going to put the ball, by watching his mannerisms, run up, and eyes. If the taker gave nothing away it was my normal practice to dive to my right. You had to make an effort, so I dived as far as I could, and it was just tough luck if the ball went the other way."

The second leg was played at Villa Park on Tuesday 5th September 1961 and a contemporary newspaper picture records the United party boarding the coach at Millmoor. Lining up from left to right in the photograph were trainer Albert Wilson, plus a thirteen man squad of players comprising Sawyer, Lambert, Kirkman, Webster, Bambridge, Waterhouse, Morgan, Weston, Ironside, Madden, Houghton, Morritt and Perry. Gordon Morritt was officially twelfth man. Brian Sawyer recalls: "Although I was injured, I went on the trip to Villa Park, basically for sentimental reasons as I played in most of the previous rounds and scored a couple of goals. No substitutes were allowed at that time, so being one of the party was just an honorary position." The club's Directors apparently shared the optimism of John Piper (mentioned above) and placed bottles of champagne on board the coach in anticipation of a famous victory. The Aston Villa match programme (price 3d) featured a team-group photograph of Rotherham United, and contained an editorial which noted: "Welcome to Rotherham, our opponents in this, the second leg of the new League Cup. We look forward to a stirring fight against this doughty Second Division outfit who have earned for themselves a great reputation as Cup-fighters." Rotherham United played the identical eleven players who had represented the club in the Millmoor leg, although Aston Villa made four changes from the first match. Looking back now, it is interesting to note how times and attitudes have changed. Peter Madden recalls: "As captain, I remember that at the kick-off we merely had the usual handshakes. There was no exchanging of pennants or mementos, and certainly the players were not allowed to swap shirts at the end of the game. We merely wore our normal League

***Left.* As an eleven year old, the author wrote to Aston Villa (enclosing a postal order and SAE) and obtained a copy of the second leg programme, for the match played on Tuesday 5th September 1961. Costing 3d at the time (1p), good condition copies now change hands for a minimum of £200. (Adrian Booth)**

kit, and it was needed for the rest of the season!" A great crowd of 31,202 witnessed the second leg and saw Aston Villa score twice to bring the aggregate scores level at ninety minutes. Heartbreakingly for the Millers, Aston Villa bagged a third in extra time to take the cup by 3-2 on aggregate.

Reporting on the sad events under a headline of 'Rotherham Not Disgraced', the *Rotherham Advertiser* dated Saturday 9th September 1961 noted: "There was no disgrace for Rotherham United in their defeat in the League Cup by Aston Villa at Villa Park on Tuesday. This was a cup tie worthy of Wembley, and a more interesting and exciting match than many of the F.A. Cup Finals played at the famous London stadium in recent years. After their 2-0 victory at Rotherham, the United lost the Cup on aggregate, Villa's win by three goals to nil swinging the total score in their favour by 3-2. After the match, Mr Joe Richards, President of the Football League and donor of the League Cup, visited the Rotherham players' dressing room and told them they had given the Cup a 'great send off in its first season'. The 'great send off' consisted of two hours of top class football played in driving rain before a crowd of 31,202, and from the noise they made, particularly when the home team were doing well, I came to the conclusion that at least 31,000 of them were shouting for the Villa. Certainly the crowd played its part in helping the Villa on to score their second goal, and both managers admitted as much to me afterwards. In assessing Rotherham's performance in this game, we must not lose sight of the fact that Villa are a famous cup winning team. They have won the F.A. Cup seven times in nine final appearances, a record challenged only by Newcastle and Blackburn Rovers with six wins each to their credit. In giving these statistics I am not

Rotherham United players in the dressing room at Villa Park prior to taking the field for the second leg of the final. Taken by A. Wilkes & Son of West Bromwich, the picture shows the team lining up with defenders at the back and forwards in front. Back row, left to right: Peter Perry, Roy Lambert, Peter Madden, Roy Ironside, Ken Waterhouse, and Lol Morgan. Front row, left to right: Barry Webster, Don Weston, Ken Houghton, Alan Kirkman and Keith Bambridge. Note the old style leather panel football. (Peter Perry collection)

Four Aston Villa players who appeared in the final, namely John Neal, Nigel Sims (who was the goalkeeper at Millmoor), Ron Wylie, and Vic Crowe. (Adrian Booth collection)

trying to minimise Rotherham's defeat. or make excuses for it. Excuses are not required for a team which can take a side of the calibre of Aston Villa into extra time for a decision to be made. Rotherham were a shade unlucky, and did not use their chances to the best advantage under trying ground conditions. Joe Richards described them as 'appalling'. When the teams took to the field they knew full well that if they could win, each player would be due for bonuses totalling over £90. It was a great incentive and one which spurred the players to put in just that little extra which adds flavour to cup ties. With so much at stake, there was no wonder both teams set about the job with determination. But this determination did not lead to doubtful tactics. On the whole, the game was cleanly fought, and the number of infringements was no larger than in a normal League match. Ken Waterhouse was prominent in Rotherham's first attack, but his pass to Houghton was cut off by John Neal, who sent Alan O'Neill away down the right wing, only to be dispossessed by Peter Madden. As the Villa continued to press, the Rotherham forwards fell back in defence. Barry Webster fell as he challenged Burrows for possession and the Rotherham defence waited for the whistle which never came. The left winger sent in a neat centre aimed at a McParland header, as Madden dropped back to clear the ball. Webster came out of a tackle on Deakin and sent the ball forward for Kirkman but the pass was a little short and Lee had no trouble in clearing the threat. Thomson broke through the Rotherham defence to lay on a good scoring chance for McParland, and Ironside brought off his first of many saves. Before the danger had been cleared, MacEwan sent in a long range shot, which landed the ball on top of the goal netting. Waterhouse, who played a stout game in defence, and prompted the attack with well judged passes, found Bambridge with a long pass but Neal moved quickly to rob the little winger as he shaped for a centre. Webster and Kirkman moved sweetly towards the Villa goal and Houghton received the final pass to kick wide of the goal as Bambridge, in a better position for a shot, waited in vain for the ball to go his way. Danger man McParland had yet another chance of making progress when he received the ball from MacEwan. Madden, who kept a tight reign on him for most of the match, sliced the ball out for an unproductive corner as McParland shot hard and accurately for goal. Morgan and Madden combined to stop Burrows as he headed for the Rotherham goal, then Kirkman was sent away for a long run on the wing, from which he gained Rotherham's first corner kick. In

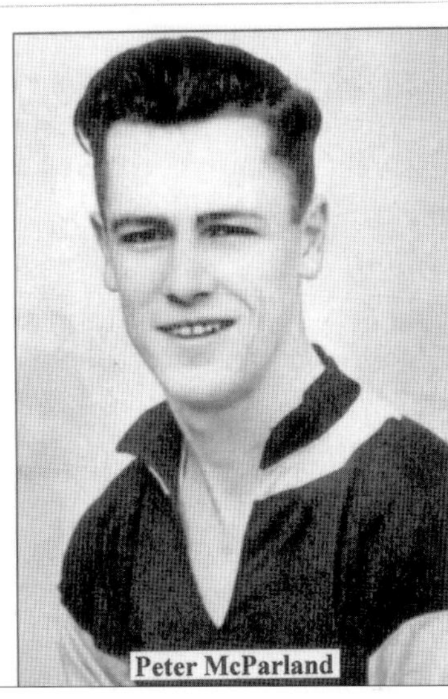

Four more Aston Villa players who appeared in the final, of who three are of great significance for Roy Ironside. Stan Lynn had his penalty kick saved by Roy; Bobby Thomson's hard shot at Millmoor led to Roy's fabulous save; whilst Peter McParland bundled the ball past Roy for a goal in the second leg. (Adrian Booth collection)

the goalmouth melee which followed, Rotherham gained a free kick on the edge of the penalty box, and Houghton lifted the ball over the bar after receiving from Waterhouse. Houghton had a good scoring chance. His first shot rebounded from a Villa defender and his second attempt was a tame affair, the ball rolling gently wide of the upright. Rotherham used the offside trap to good advantage, several promising Villa attacks being stopped through these tactics. Almost at half time Webster supplied Kirkman with the ball – and a scoring chance. The inside left sent in a full blooded left foot shot which goalkeeper Geoff Sidebottom did well to stop. The second half was almost a replica of the first, with fast end to end football and Villa having slight territorial advantage. For a long spell there seemed to be no danger of a goal being scored. Then came two shock goals for Villa – goals which threw Rotherham out of their stride. It was in the 67th minute that Villa's first goal was scored. A long centre from Deakin sent the ball high into the Rotherham penalty area. Alan O'Neill chested the ball down and flashed it into the goal as Ironside started to move out to intercept. Before Rotherham had got over the shock, left winger Burrows weaved his way through the defence and shot the ball into the goal close to the goal post. Here again was a case of the goalkeeper being unable to see wood for trees because of the number of players back in defence. Ironside was unsighted and made no effort to save. I have seen him deal competently with more difficult shots. Then Don Weston had three gilt-edged chances to save the day, but he failed miserably each time as Rotherham strove to get the odd goal. Houghton, too, had a good chance of scoring, but sent the ball wide of the goal. Webster with just the possibility of scoring sent in a fast low shot. Sidebottom blocked the ball, failed to hold on, and Houghton was given another chance. His hard shot was deflected for a corner. Morgan received the ball as it was partly cleared and started goalwards, only to be tripped on the edge of the penalty box. He took the free kick and Webster shot goalwards, but slightly wide. Lambert gathered the ball from the goal kick, sent Webster away on the right wing where he combined well with Weston to supply Kirkman with a golden opportunity. The inside man was out in front of the goal on his own and with only the goalkeeper to beat, but shot wide. The first period of extra time saw Rotherham once more pounding at the Villa goal.

Webster got through the defence and sent the ball back to Houghton, who delayed his shot and lost the ball. Then Weston got to within shooting range but sent the ball wide of goal with a miserable attempt at shooting. Ironside dived at McParland's feet to stop the centre forward getting in a close shot, and MacEwan headed over the bar in the next attack. This was football worth watching. In the twentieth minute of extra time, McParland scored a surprise goal after gathering the ball in a goalmouth melee. His snap shot sent the ball upwards, whence it slid into the net after striking the underside of the bar. After Webster had gained a corner, following a solo effort, he took the kick and placed the ball well for Kirkman to have a shot at goal. The ball beat Sidebottom, but Neal appeared as from nowhere and cleared the ball from the line. Rotherham's last despairing efforts had come to nought and the Cup had slipped from their fingers. Over to Rotherham's dressing room, where manager Tom Johnston had the last word: "It was just one of those things. The lads did well enough." he told me. Teams: Aston Villa: Sidebottom; Neal, Lee; Crowe, Dugdale, Deakin; MacEwan, O'Neill, McParland, Thomson, Burrows. Rotherham United: Ironside; Perry, Morgan; Lambert, Madden, Waterhouse; Webster, Weston, Houghton, Kirkman, Bambridge. Referee: Mr C.W. Kingston of Newport, Mon."

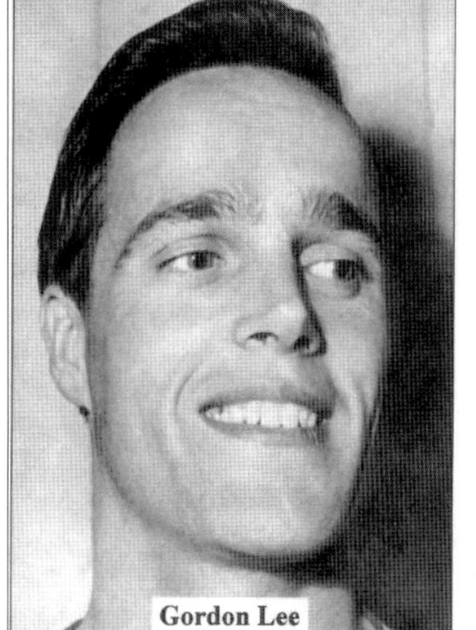
Gordon Lee

Geoff Sidebottom

Alan Deakin

Derek Dougan

A further three Aston Villa players from the final, of whom Geoff Sidebottom was the goalkeeper in the second leg at Villa Park. Derek Dougan did not play in the final, but it was he who took the champagne-filled trophy out to the Millers' players wives at Villa Park. (Adrian Booth collection)

Under a main heading of 'Rotherham lose cup – but win many plaudits' the *Sheffield Star* dated Wednesday 6th September 1961 produced a report by Basil Easterbrook, who wrote: "Rotherham United can have no complaints at failing to bring home the Football League Cup from Villa Park, but they are to be congratulated for the great rearguard action that took the First Division side into extra time. Rotherham were out powered by a physically strong team which set a furious pace from the start. McParland, recalled to Villa's attack at centre forward because Dougan was ineligible for this match, was in great form but Madden matched him with a magnificent display which must have put several thousand pounds on his value in the transfer market. I especially admired the way in which United always stayed a cohesive whole. With Villa attacks coming in constantly from all points of the compass there was never the least suggestion of panic or weakness about Rotherham's work. Even when Villa struck with two goals in two minutes at the three-quarter stage of normal time to wipe out Rotherham's two goal

THE FOOTBALL LEAGUE CUP

If at the conclusion of to-night's game a decisive result has been reached, the Trophy and Souvenirs will be presented to the teams by the donor of the Cup :

J. RICHARDS, Esq., J.P.

(President of The Football League)

31

The Football League Cup, the silver trophy purchased by Joe Richards, and presented to the captain of Aston Villa at the conclusion of the 1960/61 final. (Adrian Booth collection)

advantage gained at Millmoor in the first leg, United still worked a few breakaway chances, any one of which might have restored their lead. Weston, indeed, was guilty of a bad miss in the 78th minute and then even when McParland had got Villa's third goal in the last ten minutes of extra time, Kirkman popped up from nowhere to beat Sidebottom but alas O'Neill, back in his own penalty area, dived full length to head away what otherwise would have been a certain goal. [The *Advertiser* report said it was Neal.] Rotherham had the satisfaction of having taken part in a match that can do nothing but good for the much maligned cup. This was certainly one of the finest games that has ever been staged at Villa Park, in all its long history. Storm tossed, with rain and wind sweeping across the ground throughout the 120 minutes, there was so much incident that not one spectator in the crowd moved before the end. Rotherham certainly won the admiration of the home crowd with their tremendous display."

The trophy was presented to Aston Villa's captain by Joe Richards JP, President of the Football League and donor of the Cup, with the winning players all receiving a commemorative engraved tankard made of electro-plated nickel silver. The losing Millers players were each presented with an engraved runners-up EPNS tankard. Gordon Morritt (the Rotherham United goalkeeper) was in the dressing rooms and, speaking at his home on 1st June 2005 recalled: "I was the twelfth man at Villa Park and, after the game, I was attending to my duties, putting the dirty kit away in the skip, and generally tidying up. Joe Richards came into our dressing room with a box of runners-up tankards and thanked us for our excellent achievement in the final. He gave the box of tankards to Tom Johnston, who went round and gave one to each player. There were twelve, and the last one was given by Tom to our trainer Albert Wilson. As I was sorting out the skips, I came upon the bottles of champagne which we had brought down with us, but one of the Directors refused to let us drink it as we had lost. Just at this moment Joe Mercer, the Aston Villa manager, came into our dressing room to thank us for a good game, and he saw me putting the champagne back into our skip. He asked me to go with him, and we walked through into the Villa dressing room. There he presented me with a few bottles of Villa's champagne for our lads. He also asked me if I had got a tankard and, when I replied no, he said that they had one spare and gave it to me. It has the F.A. emblem on and is silver plated. Thus I am the only Rotherham United player who owns an Aston Villa tankard!" As will be noted, Gordon remembers there being twelve tankards for Rotherham United, presumably as they had only used eleven players over the two legs of the final. Aston Villa used fifteen players over the two legs, and presumably they received more tankards, resulting in the 'spare' being available for Gordon. Peter Madden remembers an interesting fact about the presentations: "The winners' tankards all had lids on, whereas our runners-up tankards were just plain." Speaking on 5th May 2005, Ken Houghton also recalled the aftermath: "The tankards were in a box with a blue velvet lining. After the match, the Aston Villa team were all drinking champagne and singing in their dressing room and they kindly sent some of their bubbly round to our dressing room." Speaking on 14th April 2005, Roy Lambert laughed as he remembered the incident: "We had our bottles of champagne waiting in a skip in the dressing room but, when the Villa lads sent us some of their champagne, the Rotherham directors couldn't get our bottles back into the team bus quick enough!" At some stage in the proceedings the trophy found its way outside the ground, leading to a humorous and fondly remembered incident which was recalled by Dorothy Waterhouse (Ken Waterhouse's wife) at their home near Lancaster on 11th March 2005: "Four of the players wives had travelled down for the match in Lol Morgan's car. Pauline Morgan did the driving, and Dorian Kettleborough, Anne Perry and myself were passengers. We had complimentary tickets and watched the match from the stand, but afterwards we had to wait outside the player's entrance for our husbands. Suddenly the Cup was brought out to us by Derek Dougan [who by then had moved to Aston Villa but was 'cup-tied' for the final]. The cup was filled with champagne and we all had a drink out of it!" This incident is also recalled by Anne Perry. Ken Houghton takes up the story: "On our coach journey back to Rotherham, because we had lost, our Directors still refused to open up the champagne that was stowed back on board." When asked to comment on this, Peter Madden confirmed: "That is definitely true and in fact there was quite a frosty atmosphere on that return journey".

When asked on 15th April 2005 to recall his memories of the second leg, Peter Perry simply quipped: "I just remember it was lashing down with rain throughout the match!" Brian Sawyer recalls: "I was not presented with the twelfth runners-up tankard, however, as for some reason manager Tom Johnston decided that trainer Albert Wilson should have it. Incidentally, I did play away at Darlington a few days after the final. It was a big mistake, as my knee collapsed again and I never regained full fitness". The match referred to by Brian Sawyer, away at Darlington, was played on Monday 11th September 1961. Only six days after the second leg of the final, that match at Feethams marked the first round of the 1961/62 League Cup competition! In the match programme, under the heading of 'Club Jottings', the Darlington editor wrote: "Tonight we take time off from Fourth Division duties to partake in an extra tit-bit on the Feethams menu. All supporters will extend a warm welcome to Rotherham United, old friends who pay us this long-awaited return visit in the first round of the League Cup competition. Rotherham are the losing finalists from last year's League Cup having lost on a 3-2 aggregate to Aston Villa in the long delayed final which, unlike the early rounds, is played on a home and away basis. We had hoped that they would win and bring the Cup with them tonight." Amen to that.

The victorious Aston Villa players admire the cup and celebrate their victory with glasses of champagne, some of which was passed through into the Millers dressing room, as related in the text. Note the embroidered towels incorporating the club name. (Daily Mail)

6. Players' Appearances and Goal Scorers

In the run to the cup final the maximum possible number of appearances by any one Rotherham United player was eight, in the games versus Leicester City (won 2-1), Bristol Rovers (won 2-0), Bolton Wanderers (won 2-0), Portsmouth (won 3-0), Shrewsbury Town (won 4-3 over two legs) and Aston Villa (lost 2-3 over two legs). No substitutes were allowed in that era (and were only introduced in season 1965/66, and then just one allowed in case of injury) giving a cup run total of 88 player appearances and fifteen goals. Rotherham United used sixteen players in the tournament.

Player's name	Appearances	Goals scored
Roy Ironside	8	
Peter Perry	8	
Lol Morgan	8	
Roy Lambert	8	
Keith Bambridge	7	
Alan Kirkman	7	3
Peter Madden	7	
Ken Waterhouse	7	
Ken Houghton	6	3
Barry Webster	6	1
Brian Sawyer	5	2
Don Weston	5	3
Brian Jackson	2	
Keith Kettleborough	2	1
George Darwin	1	1
Eddie O'Hara	1	
Syd Farrimond (Bolton, own goal)		1
Total:	88	15

With the obvious exception of the great Dave Watson, photographs showing ex-Rotherham United players in a full international England squad are somewhat thin on the ground, so this picture is both rare and interesting. It depicts an England squad being coached by Sir Alf Ramsey (second right) with Keith Kettleborough seen in the centre. Other players include, left to right: Barry Bridges (9), Terry Paine (7), Ken Shellito, Nobby Stiles, Bobby Charlton, John Kaye (arms folded), Bobby Moore (6), Derek Temple and Ray Wilson (3). When shown this photograph, Keith commented: "The picture was taken at the Bank of England Ground at Hendon, and we were staying at the Hendon Hall Hotel, prior to a match versus Austria. I attended all the training sessions, but unfortunately did not make Ramsey's final eleven." The match was played at Wembley on 20th October 1965 and perhaps England could have done with some Rotherham 'steel' that night; England were twice ahead through Bobby Charlton and John Connelly, but two late goals gave Austria a 3-2 win. (Soccer Star)

7. Players Who Appeared in the Final

Rotherham United fielded the identical eleven players in both legs of the first final. The famous First Finalists were:

Roy Ironside (goalkeeper)
Roy is considered by many supporters to be Rotherham United's best-ever goalkeeper and was (and he still is) known to his team mates as 'Big Iron'. He was born in the Heeley district of Sheffield on 28th May 1935 and, upon leaving school at the age of fifteen, took up employment as an apprentice fitter at the Atlas & Norfolk works. Speaking on 9th June 2005 at the home of Barry Webster, his great friend of over fifty years, Roy recalled: "I began playing goalkeeper for the Atlas & Norfolk Under 16 team and one of my team mates was Melvyn Hooper, who was the son of the Rotherham United trainer Mark Hooper [the former Sheffield Wednesday player who played outside right, and scored, in their 1935 F.A. Cup Final victory]. Melvyn told his dad about me, and he came to watch me play, along with Joe McGuire, the Millers scout. I signed as an amateur in 1952, but at that time Rotherham had five goalkeepers and I played as a junior in the A team in the Yorkshire League." Roy made steady progress at Millmoor, however, and signed as a part-time professional in July 1954, although there was still serious competition for a first team spot, with the famous John Quairney holding the jersey. Roy recalls: "In July 1956 I was called up for my National Service, and joined the Royal Electrical & Mechanical Engineers (REME) at Honiton for six weeks initial training. I was then posted to Bordon in Hampshire where I passed out as an armaments fitter. While there I played in goal for my Regiment when we twice won the British Army Cup, and I also played for the British Army. The first time we won the cup the presentations were made by Her Majesty Queen Elizabeth 11. My team mates then included Bobby Charlton, Mel Charles and Bill Currie the former Brighton and Derby player. I came out of the Army in July 1958 and immediately signed as a full-time professional for Rotherham United." In fact Roy had made his full League debut during season 1956/57, when a spell of home leave allowed him to keep a clean sheet in the 1-0 home win versus Stoke City on 16th February 1957. Roy played spasmodically over the next two seasons, still in competition with John Quairney, but 1959/60 saw him as first team goalkeeper from the opening match. He only missed one League and Cup game throughout the whole campaign, playing a vital role in the epic F.A. Cup saga versus Arsenal and Brighton & Hove Albion. His growing reputation resulted in Liverpool expressing an interest in signing him, but they were rebuffed. Roy stayed with Rotherham United until season 1964/65, when he made just four first team appearances as Gordon Morritt had taken over the green jersey. Roy's somewhat ignominious farewell appearance was on 21st November 1964 in the crashing 1-6 away defeat at Southampton. Altogether he had clocked-up 220 League games and 32 cup ties for the club.

Roy Ironside, the history-making United goalkeeper who saved the first ever penalty to be taken in a League Cup final. (Adrian Booth collection)

Peter Perry (right back)
Peter was a sturdy and confident full back who is widely remembered as United's penalty taking expert in the early 1960s. He was born in Treeton, near Rotherham, on 11th April 1936 and his first significant football experience came when – aged 15 – he had one season at junior level with Sheffield Wednesday, as an outside right. This was arranged by Doug Witcombe of Sheffield Wednesday. He then joined Treeton Reading Room FC who played in the Rotherham & District Under 18 League and also signed for Rotherham United as an amateur in 1953/54. Speaking at his home on 15th April 2005 Peter recalled: "At this time I frequently played two matches on Saturdays. I would play inside-left for United Juniors on Saturday morning in the Northern Intermediate League (often played at Dinnington), then went home for a bite to eat before turning out for Treeton Reading Room on Saturday afternoon!" In this era the Juniors were drawn against Manchester United Juniors in a

Peter Perry takes a penalty kick against Ipswich Town on 5th March 1960, as Keith Kettleborough looks on in the right background. The ball is about to hit the wrist of goalkeeper Roy Bailey and fly over the bar, but Peter never again missed from the spot. The muddy pitch highlights the conditions in which players were expected to perform in that era, as discussed in the introduction. (Peter Perry collection)

cup match and Peter remembers: "The game was played at Millmoor and there was a good crowd. David Pegg was playing for Manchester United and the match finished 0-0. We travelled over for the replay which was played at The Cliff in Salford and, when we were warming up, one of our team remarked about a big fella who had trotted out in the Manchester United team. It turned out to be Duncan Edwards, who proved to be far too good for us and he scored a hat-trick as Manchester won 3-0." Peter was then called up for his National Service and went in the Army from 1954 to 1956, saying: "I served in the 2nd Training Regiment of the Royal Signals, based at Catterick, where I rose to the rank of Corporal. During this period I was picked for every game played by the Regiment, a highlight being our run to the Army Cup final in 1956. This match was played at Aldershot and we won 3-1 versus the Argyll & Sutherland Highlanders, with the Cup being presented by the Rt. Hon. Anthony Eden. A team mate in that final was Brian Slater who played for Rotherham United, Grimsby Town and Sheffield Wednesday." [Brian Slater played seventeen games for the Millers in 1956/57.] When Peter came out of the Army he was able to sign for Rotherham United in July 1956 but stressed: "I would only sign as a part-time professional because, throughout my time at Millmoor, I worked as a clerk at the United Coke & Chemical Company's works at Orgreave, where I stayed until I retired. I had a great boss, however, who knew all about my football and gave me time off work whenever I needed it for mid-week training, mid-week games, or to travel to long distance away games. All he asked was that, if I missed time in the week, then I would make up the hours on Saturday morning or on Sunday. I always trained Tuesday and Thursday mornings with the first team, plus four evenings along with Keith Bambridge and Lol Morgan. Our normal day-time training involved lapping the Millmoor pitch, sprinting, and running up and down the terracing. Then we usually finished off with a game on the area of land behind the goal at the scrap yard end. In those days it was an area of red shale and we had some tremendous hard-fought games, with no quarter given. It was a cup final every day down there! Later on, of course, the club built the gymnasium on the red shale area. On occasions we would have a change of routine and go training on Herringthorpe Playing Fields." Peter made his first team debut for the Millers, aged 22, in the last game of the 1957/58 season and still recalls it vividly, noting: "the game was a mid-week night match [on Thursday 1st May 1958, kick off at 6-30pm] down at Fulham and Andy Smailes was the manager. George Cohen and Jimmy Hill were playing for Fulham, and I played right back and marked Chamberlain. Unfortunately we lost 1-3, with David Layne scoring our goal." He also clearly recalls his first home match for Rotherham, which was a 4-3 victory over Charlton Athletic on Thursday 28th August 1958. By this time Peter was established at right back and in fact every one of the 99 League and 19 cup tie appearances he made for the club was in this position. Peter tells a lovely story about one of his games for the Millers: "We played away at Sunderland [28th November 1959] and won 2-1, with me marking England international Colin Grainger who was playing outside left. Sunderland took a corner on their right wing and the ball was headed out by one of our defenders. Colin Grainger ran in from the left and met the ball on the edge of our box and blasted in a first time shot. I was coming off our line and the ball hit me full in the face. I never saw it coming and was seeing stars afterwards. Next day it said in the paper that I had made a brilliant goal line clearance!" Peter is, of course, recalled as the Millers' ice-cool penalty taking expert and is widely remembered as the man who never missed. When asked about his spot kick technique, however, he remarked: "Ah yes, but I did miss the first one I ever took for Rotherham United. It was in a match against Ipswich Town [on 5th March 1960] when the score was 0-0. I hit the ball hard and high to goalkeeper Roy Bailey's right, but unfortunately the ball hit his wrist and spun up over the crossbar and out for a corner. We ended up losing that match 1-4. But after that I never missed again. In those days goalkeepers had to remain stationary in the middle of their goal and could not move until the ball was actually struck. My technique was therefore to hit the ball with the inside of my foot, fairly hard and low, and aimed to hit the side netting just inside the bottom of the post. Even if the goalkeeper guessed the right way, there was not time for him to dive right down to the foot of his post before the ball was in the back of the net." Records reveal that Peter's first successful conversion was on 1st October 1960 at Millmoor in a 2-1 win versus Leyton Orient, and that he netted twelve out of twelve penalties taken after that first miss. All his first team goals were spot kicks. Asked if he got nervous when taking penalties, he replied: "No, I never worried and the crowd never got to me. In fact I enjoyed taking them." Back in the early 1960s it was rare for players to have their own transport and Peter recalls those times with some affection: "None of we players had our own cars and we all travelled to matches and training on public transport. For home games I used to catch the number 132 bus from Treeton and then walked up from town to Millmoor. I would always be recognised and enjoyed walking up with the fans, chatting about the previous week's game and the prospects for the day's match. When we arrived at the Millmoor Hotel there was always one dedicated supporter in that area who I can clearly remember to this day. He was a badly disabled gentleman who could not walk, and he used to get to games by using a stool, which he pushed along the pavement dragging his legs behind him. The sheer physical effort that man put in to get to matches must have been incredible!" [*author's note*: on my own visits to Millmoor in those days I also saw this disabled gentleman, but had forgotten about him until Peter brought back to me a forty-five year old memory.] Returning to Peter's story, he recalled: "Other players came to games on public transport. For example Keith Bambridge always bussed in, and Roy Ironside and Barry Webster used to come together on the bus from Sheffield."

Lol Morgan (left back)

Lawrence Morgan (always known as Lol) is recalled as a determined and resolute tackler, and his debut in season 1954/55 meant that he was the longest-serving Millers player who played in the League Cup final. He was born in the Eastwood area of Rotherham on 5th May 1931. Speaking at his home on 14th April 2005 he recalled: "I started my football career at the age of 15 when, in 1946, I joined Sheffield United as a junior and played in the Blades 'A' team in the Yorkshire League. This came about because my uncle Albert Nightingale was a Sheffield United player and he made the arrangements. Albert was transferred to Huddersfield Town [he played there from season 1947/48 to 1951/52] and later arranged for me to go and join him. I signed as a part-time player at Huddersfield Town in March 1949 on a wage of £5 per

An early portrait of Lol Morgan, the long serving Millers left back, seen here in the white away kit. Lol Morgan autographed the picture in 2006. (Adrian Booth collection)

week. At this time I was also an apprentice electrician at the British Oxygen Company in Rotherham. I did training on my own in the evenings and went over to Huddersfield just for matches, travelling on the bus from Rotherham to Chapeltown, and then changing on to the Sheffield to Huddersfield bus. While I was with Huddersfield Town I did my two years National Service, served in the Royal Air Force, and signed as a full-time professional at the end of this. George Darwin was also at Huddersfield Town while I was there. I played seven games in their first team." [The book *Huddersfield Town – 75 Years On* by George Binns, published by Huddersfield Town FC in 1984, confirms that Lol played seven games for Town, all at left-half, with six games in 1949/50 and one in 1950/51.] Lol's first-class debut for Huddersfield Town was in October 1949 in a home game versus Aston Villa which was won 1-0. Lol continues his story by recalling: "Huddersfield Town had a change of manager when Andy Beattie, an ex-Preston North End player and Scottish international, took over. He gave me a free transfer, and so I took the opportunity to move to Rotherham United in August 1954. At that time Rotherham had over forty professionals and I remember being given boot peg number 42." [Andy Beattie was manager of Huddersfield Town from 1952 to 1956 and was succeeded there by Bill Shankly.] With all that competition for first team positions at Rotherham, newcomer Lol made just four appearances, still at left-half, in his first two seasons at Millmoor, with his first team debut in a 3-0 win versus Port Vale at home on 11th December 1954. By 1956/57 he had settled in at left back and made the position his own, although Lol felt that the life of a full-time professional footballer was not quite enough for him, commenting: "We used to train in the mornings and then spend most of our afternoons playing snooker. I decided to get another job and applied for and got a post with the *Rotherham Advertiser* which involved me travelling around the area visiting people and companies selling advertising space." Defending was Lol's forte, as indicated by the strange fact that, in his 326 games for Rotherham United, he did not once appear on the score sheet! When asked about this on 14th April 2005, Lol smiled and commented: "Yes it's true that I never scored a single goal in my entire professional career. I never even hit the woodwork. The nearest I ever came to scoring was in a game versus Manchester City when I got an effort on target and thought it was going in. I was just about to start my celebrations when their goalkeeper made a fabulous save and flicked the ball round the post. In my days with Rotherham United we always played the old-fashioned three man defence with Peter Madden at centre half and myself and Peter Perry pivoting as full-backs. If Peter went up field, I would pivot back slightly behind Peter, and vice versa. But I was never very inclined to go forward and possibly this goes back to a rather forceful coach in my early days who, in brusque Yorkshire tones once told me: 'You see this white line across the middle of the pitch? I don't want you to cross it'. With three at the back at Rotherham I was always conscious of my defensive responsibilities but, when the 4-4-2 formation became more formalised, that always left two central defenders at the back and gave a little bit more leeway for the person playing in my left back position to push forward." As mentioned in the Introduction, Lol marked England international Stanley Matthews in the well known game versus Stoke City at Millmoor on Saturday 16th December 1961. Matthews played his first League game in March 1932, was known as the 'Wizard of Dribble' (although he also had a fine turn of pace) and played his last game on 6th February 1965 when aged 50 years and 5 days. Asked on 6th August 2005 for his recollections of playing against the wing maestro, Lol said: "I remember the Stoke match well. Stanley Matthews did not do a lot that day. His pace had disappeared by then, so he never tried to take me on for speed. When he received the ball, he just did a little wiggle of the hips and knocked the ball inside. Unfortunately he did score against me. The ball was played across the penalty area, inside me, and Matthews hit it with his left foot. The ground was very hard that day and, although the ball was not hit with much power, it bobbled badly and went over Roy Ironside's hand and ended up in the net. I was a bit upset as I don't think Matthews had ever used his left foot before that match!" Alan Kirkman also recalls the game and, speaking on 11th August 2005, said: "when Matthews received the ball he was looking to lay it off inside, and he did not really have much impact on the game apart from the fluke goal". By season 1963/64 Lol was still cemented into the left back role and made forty first team appearances that campaign. The summer of 1964 gave him a change of direction when he moved to Darlington, as discussed later, and his last-ever game for the Millers was on 25th April 1964 in the 0-0 draw away at Plymouth Argyle. Altogether Lol made an impressive 291 League and 35 Cup appearances for United – even if he never did get on the score sheet!

Roy Lambert (right half)
Roy will be forever remembered as a true stalwart of Rotherham United, playing year after year, captaining the team at one time, and proving to be a fine tactician out on the park. Speaking at his home in Swinton on 10th June 2005, Roy recounts: "I was born at Hoyland Common on 16th July 1933, but only lived there a few months before my family moved into a pit house at Warren, near Chapeltown. The major employer in the area was the well known firm of Newton Chambers and my dad worked at one of their pits, Barley Hall Colliery near Thorpe. I attended High Green School and played for the school football team but left aged fourteen. I worked for one year in the foundry at Newton Chambers, before following dad down Barley Hall Colliery." Roy quickly won a place in the company football team, Thorncliffe Welfare, and they reached a cup final in May 1954 which was watched by the Rotherham United manager Andy Smailes. Roy recalls: "After the final, Andy Smailes asked to see me and offered to sign me for

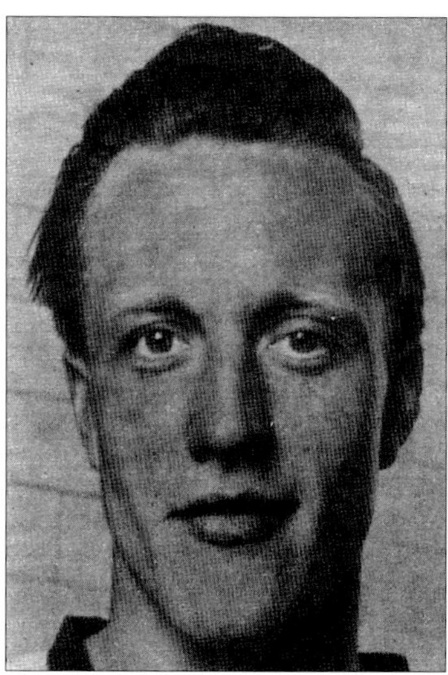

Roy Lambert, photographed about 1961. (Adrian Booth collection)

Rotherham United. I told him that I could not sign, as I was about to be called up. Nevertheless, he said he would like to sign me on part-time terms and so I signed the following day and was given a £10 signing-on fee." He was duly called-up for a spell of National Service and, in July 1954, reported to Hillsea Barracks in Portsmouth. Roy continued: "After initial training I was posted to Egypt, and played for the Army against the RAF and the Egypt Olympic X1. One of my team mates was the Everton winger Derek Mayers. Upon my return from Egypt in April 1956 I was posted to Ashchurch, near Tewkesbury, and there played for my regiment when we won a cup final." Upon his demob from the Army in July 1956, Roy returned to Millmoor and signed as a full time professional. He was an old fashioned wing half by trade, being a tough tackler but with a good football brain, and had a long and illustrious career for United. He recalls: "At first I played in the Reserves, and my first game for the first team was a County Cup game away at Doncaster Rovers which was a 0-0 draw. On Saturday 12th January 1957 I played for the Reserves away at Nottingham Forest and we won 5-2 with me scoring two goals. I was then promoted to the first team and, by a great coincidence, made my full League debut the following Saturday, again away at Nottingham Forest. We lost 1-3 and I was up against international Eddie Bailey. I then kept my first team place and in my next two games faced two more internationals, Johnny Haynes of Fulham and Ivor Allchurch of Swansea Town. It was a tough start, but I kept my place and altogether played thirteen games on the trot." He actually found out about his League debut in unusual circumstances, as he recounts: "I had been training at Millmoor and then popped down into the Rotherham town centre. As I was going for my bus home, I noticed it was about to leave and hastily bought a *Sheffield Star* newspaper and just managed to jump on to the back platform of the bus as it was setting off. I found out on the back page of the paper that I had been chosen for the Forest game, and my dad was really pleased when I showed him the news. But I had only been with manager Andy Smailes a couple of hours before, and he never said a word to me!" Roy netted his first senior goal on 19th April 1957 in a 3-3 draw away at Lincoln City, and it was a collector's item, for Roy was renowned as a resolute defender and scored just six career goals for the Millers! Roy remembers the goal well: "As a centre came in, I jumped up for the ball and just managed to flick it into the net as their goalkeeper challenged and gave me a painful punching on the head!" Roy's very last appearance in the red shirt came in the 1-0 away win at Bury on 27th April 1965 and he remembers: "The manager by this time was Jack Mansell. He called me into his office one day and told me that he was going to bring the youngsters on and that I would be playing in the Reserves from then on. I never played a single League game under Mansell." Roy made 307 League and 39 Cup appearances for Rotherham United.

Andy Smailes

Peter Madden (centre half and Captain)

For several seasons Peter Madden was the Millers skipper, and was described by manager Tom Johnston as being: "A born leader". Madden was born in Bradford on 31st October 1934 and started out playing for Thornton Juniors in local Bradford soccer. Speaking at his home near Rochdale on 11th March 2005, Peter explained how Rotherham United came to sign him, saying: "I had done my National Service in the Coldstream Guards and after returning home I signed for amateur side Thackley. My uncle thought I was good enough to make it in the professional game and told scout Joe McGuire about me, and Joe soon arranged a trial with Rotherham United. I then signed on a part-time basis in October 1955." Peter played just one League game in season 1955/56, at left back in the 1-3 defeat away at Plymouth Argyle on 14th April 1956.

was against his old club Preston North End! This was in the 3-1 home win on 16th March 1963 when two of his protégés – Bennett (2) and Butler – scored the goals. Altogether Ken Waterhouse made 123 League and 20 cup appearances for the Millers, scoring 12 League and one cup goals.

Barry Webster (outside right)
John Barry Webster was a speedy winger and will retain a permanent place in football history for scoring the first ever goal netted in a Football League Cup final. During his time at Millmoor he was a big favourite with the home crowd and was affectionately nicknamed 'cowboy' due to the shape of his legs! Barry was born on 3rd March 1935 in the Greenhill area of Sheffield, although his family soon moved to Meersbrook. Speaking at his home in Sheffield on 9th June 2005, Barry recalled: "I joined Sheffield Club when only sixteen years of age and initially played for their reserves in the Association League. After just three games I was promoted to the first team, playing on the right wing, and one of the youngest players in the Yorkshire League. In 1953 I was called up for my National Service in the 3rd Signals Regiment and served 22 months out in Egypt. There I played for the British Army and also for the Combined Services versus Egypt at the Olympic Stadium." After his two years were completed Barry signed for Gainsborough Trinity, who were managed by the former Sheffield United player Sammy Thorpe, and played in the Midland League. Rotherham United manager Andy Smailes went along to one Trinity match and promptly offered Barry part time terms, as he recalls: "Andy signed me for Rotherham, with training on Tuesday and Thursday nights. Strangely enough, my very first game for United Reserves was against

Barry Webster, the history-making United winger who scored the first ever goal in a League Cup final. Barry autographed this picture at a players' reunion at Kimberworth on 19th March 2005. (Adrian Booth collection)

Gainsborough Trinity, and I scored a goal! During season 1956/57 I scored over a dozen goals for the Reserves." He played his first League game for the club on 1st September 1956 in the 0-2 home reversal to Blackburn Rovers, and comments: "On my debut I played right wing and was marked by England international left back Bill Eckersley. He gave me a hard time. I was a novice then. That season I just played four games for the first team as my rival for the number 7 shirt was Jack Grainger, a Rotherham United legend." Barry won the number 7 position, however, and for the next five seasons he was virtually an ever-present and was the leading goal scorer in two of those campaigns. Living in Sheffield, he used to travel to training and matches on the number 69 bus, along with his great pal of over fifty years, Roy Ironside. Barry recalls: "None of the players had cars in those days, and it was just accepted that you travelled to games on the bus, along with the fans. I remember when we had the famous second replay of the cup-tie versus Arsenal at Hillsborough, Roy and me went together on the tram up to Hillsborough!" Barry almost left the Millers at one time, commenting: "Liverpool had me watched and put in a bid of £10,000, which was matched by Sheffield United. But I very nearly signed for Derby County and got as far as visiting Derby to look at a house. At this time Brian Sawyer badly injured his knee and the club decided they could not release me." One of the highlights of Barry's career was scoring the Millers' goal in the drawn F.A. Cup match, away at Arsenal before a crowd of 57,598. Asked who his toughest opponent was in that era, Barry replied: "Kenny Malcolm of Ipswich Town was the best left back I ever played against. I had tough games down there, although I have to say that they had great turf on the Portman Road pitch." Barry's last appearance in the red shirt came in the final match of 1961/62, on 28th April 1962 in the 3-0 away win at Huddersfield Town. That game also marked his last goal for the club. At the end of the season he was released, having played in 179 League games and 22 cup-ties for Rotherham United, scoring 37 League and four cup goals, whilst also carving out a niche for himself in national football cup history. Speaking of his time at Millmoor, Barry recalls: "There is nothing quite like your first professional club and I loved every minute of my time at Rotherham United. We had a lovely bunch of players who generally all got on great together, stayed at each other's houses after long-haul trips, socialised together, and represented the club at many supporters social gatherings. All our wives and girlfriends seemed to get on well together too. They were great days."

Don Weston (inside right)
Don's speed as a forward has been commented upon by several of his former colleagues. Brian Sawyer observed: "Don had the acceleration and speed over the first few yards that is the most devastating as a footballer." Keith Bambridge recalled: "He was lightening fast", and this sentiment is also held by strike partner Ken Houghton who remarked: "Don had a wonderful burst of speed". Roy Ironside also came up with a lovely quote about Don, saying: "He could catch pigeons!" Don was born in Mansfield on 6th March 1936 and, in his younger days, represented East Derbyshire Boys. Speaking at his home near Mansfield on 2nd January 2005 he recalled: "I was called up for National Service and joined the army in June 1956, being posted to 31 Training Regiment Royal Artillery in North Wales. I played in services football and was spotted by a Wrexham scout who arranged for me to have a trial. I also had a trial at West Bromwich Albion around this time. After my stint in the army I signed as a professional for Wrexham." After 42 League games (21 goals) for the Welshmen, Don moved to Birmingham City when Wrexham were unable to resist an offer of £14,000 for their striker. Don only played 23 League games for the Midlands outfit, scoring three goals. The *Rotherham Advertiser* dated 23rd December 1960 reported: "Last night, Rotherham United paid the club's highest-ever fee for a player, to Birmingham City, for the transfer of centre-forward Don Weston. The fee involved was a five-figure amount, believed to be around the £10,000 mark. Birmingham paid Fourth Division Wrexham £14,000 for the player ten months ago. Weston, who is 24, and a full-time professional, was a prolific goal scorer with Wrexham, but was unable to maintain his scorching marksmanship after moving to the Midlands. In 16 appearances for City's first team last season he scored three goals. This season, in seven First Division appearances, he has failed to score. His last appearance with the Birmingham senior side was on November 5th, after which he was relegated to the reserves. But both Don Weston and Rotherham manager Mr Tom Johnston are hoping the player will regain his scoring streak with the move to Millmoor. For both the player and Rotherham United badly need goals. At his best, Weston can provide them, and it may be that the transition to the First Division in one mighty jump was too much for him. The Second Division might be more to his liking. Although United have been keeping an eye on Weston for some time, it was not until after mid-day yesterday that the transfer deal really began to warm up. After a phone call from Birmingham, Mr Johnston headed south, and several hours later rang club chairman, Mr M.R. Cooper to confirm 'I have signed Weston'. United's secretary Mr L. Holmes, although unable to disclose the fee, confirmed it was the highest in the club's history for an incoming player." Don made his Rotherham first team debut at centre forward in the daunting Boxing Day clash at Anfield, where a crowd of over 39,000 saw Liverpool win 2-1. He was an ever-present for the rest of the season, and scored his first goal for Rotherham in his second match, the return fixture versus Liverpool on 27th December 1960 which the Millers won 1-0. Weston went on the Rotherham United tour of Finland after the end of the 1960/61 season and was one of three United players who played for Aliance. Don's last match for the club was in the 1-4 defeat away at Newcastle United on 8th December 1962, giving him an overall record of 74 League games for Rotherham United, in which he scored 23 goals. Don recalled: "I never really liked it at Birmingham City and was glad to be able to sign for Rotherham United where there was a friendly bunch of players. I enjoyed my time at Rotherham very much, but it was too big a chance to miss to move on to a big club like Leeds United."

Don Weston, the centre forward who arrived from Birmingham City in exchange for the Millers' then record transfer outlay, and later moved on for a successful spell with Leeds United. The picture was autographed by Don on 2nd January 2005. (Adrian Booth collection)

Ken Houghton (centre forward)
Ken is remembered for his exceptional ball control, while packing an explosive shot, and was noted for rifling in some spectacular long-range goals. Kenneth Houghton was born in Rotherham on 18th October

Ken Houghton played in both legs of the final, but soon moved on to Hull City in a 'big money' transfer. He became a big favourite with Tigers fans, as part of the legendary Butler, Chilton, Houghton and Wagstaff forward line, and was later the club manager. Ken autographed the picture on 5th May 2005. (Soccer Star)

1939, and lived on Mallory Road, East Herringthorpe, along with his two sisters and four brothers. He attended Spurley Hey School and played for the school team. He always harboured the dream of being a professional footballer, but coal mining was in the family blood and he left school at 15 and took a job with the National Coal Board. Speaking on 5th May 2005 at his home in Hull, Ken recalled: "I signed up for the NCB at Silverwood Colliery, which was just over the hill from our house, but initially was sent to the Area Training Centre at Manvers to be taught about the job. One of the things we had to do was learn about pit ponies and I was shown how to harness and lead ponies. After my initial training I went back to Silverwood Colliery as a trainee underground worker and eventually progressed to working on the coal face. It was normal practice for the NCB to place families together, so I found myself working with three of my brothers as members of a twenty strong team on a stall." Ken went on to mention a little remembered fact, that he could have become a Blades star, revealing: "I started out with Sheffield United, and played two years as a centre forward for their Juniors in the Northern Intermediate League. It was fairly heavy going, however, as I had to go training at Sheffield on Tuesday and Thursday evenings. This involved me doing my shift at the pit, then going on two buses to Sheffield, doing my training, catching two buses back, and then be off again to the pit the following morning." Circumstances suddenly altered at Sheffield United, however, as Ken went on to explain: "I was starting to make a breakthrough and had played a few games for their Reserves with Joe Mercer as Manager and Dick Taylor as coach, who both took an interest in my progress. However, they moved on to Aston Villa and, in the uncertain period leading up to the Blades getting a new manager, I got a bit fed up of the situation and the travelling and left. I signed-on for the Silverwood Colliery team and played at centre half for them." Things then changed for the better for Ken, as a Rotherham United scout quickly spotted him in action for the pit team and, in March 1960, he signed for the Millers, initially as an amateur. He was quickly recognised as being a great prospect and, by the start of season 1960/61, Rotherham United had him signed as a full-time professional and he left the coal mining industry. The Rotherham United versus Bristol Rovers programme dated 23rd November 1960, in a section detailing goal scorers to date, noted that Houghton had already scored 21 goals for the second team. Ken explained how he rapidly established himself by recalling: "I played centre forward in the Reserves where I got five hat-tricks in my first nine games, and was quickly promoted to the first team. I can vividly remember my League debut, which was against Middlesbrough at Millmoor [on 3rd September 1960, when Rotherham United lost 1-2] and I was put on the right wing. Marking me was England international full back Mick McNeil and, playing in a strange position against a class player, I didn't get a kick! The following Monday I received a message that I was to report to manager Tom Johnston's office and, fearing the worst, I thought he was going to tell me I was out. However, Tom told me he had plans to give me half a dozen games at centre forward to prove myself." [the six consecutive games were in November and December.] Ken continued: "After that run in the first team I never looked back. One particularly happy memory I have is of scoring a hat trick versus Bury at Millmoor." [a 6-2 win played on 14th December 1963] Between season 1960/61 and 1964/65 Ken made 149 League and 27 cup appearances for the Millers, netting an impressive 56 League and 11 cup goals. His last first team game was on 28th December 1964 in the 1-1 home draw versus Derby County. Ken Houghton was a class act and it was hardly surprising that scouts from various clubs were sniffing around Millmoor, amongst them being Cliff Britton the Hull City manager who had made the signing of Houghton a top priority.

Alan Kirkman (inside left)
Alan was capable of playing in most of the forward positions, but is remembered as a crafty inside forward with an eye for goal, and an excellent header of the ball. Alan is a Lancastrian, having been born in Bolton on 21st June 1936. By the time he was seventeen years of age he was playing for Bacup Borough in the Lancashire Combination League. He quickly gained local representative honours when chosen to play for the Lancashire

A contemporary portrait of Alan Kirkham, which appeared as card number 8 in a series of footballers issued by C.S. Ltd. of Slough. (Adrian Booth collection)

FA team and, in that game, he was spotted by a Manchester City scout. Speaking at his home on 11th March 2005, Alan recalled: "I had a trial at Maine Road and firstly signed amateur forms for Manchester City in 1954, and then signed professional in February 1956. I was mainly in the reserves at City, as they had some good forwards at that time such as Don Revie, Joe Hayes, Bobby Johnstone and Jack Dyson. I made my first team debut at Birmingham City [in the last match of season 1956/57 on 27th April 1957] and scored two goals in a 3-3 draw. In my second match, at Hillsborough against Sheffield Wednesday [a 5-4 win for City on 21st December 1957. Tony Kay and Peter Swan were playing for the Owls.] I scored a hat-trick, but still could not hold down a regular first team place. In some published records I am only shown as scoring two goals against Sheffield Wednesday but I definitely got a hat trick. For my third, I got in a header and am certain it had crossed the line before Bobby Johnstone got a touch. He was credited with the goal, but I am certain to this day that it was mine!" In fact Alan only made seven first team appearances for Manchester City, in which he scored six goals! Alan went on to say: "In season 1958/59 I was getting itchy feet, wanting first team football, and wondering whether to leave City. I talked this over with the first team trainer, who advised me to bide my time as my chance would come in the first team, but how long do you wait?" So when Tom Johnston came in for Kirkman, saying he needed someone to pep up the Millers' first team attack, Alan decided to take the plunge. He moved over the Pennines and signed-on at Millmoor for a fee of £4,000, scoring on his debut (playing at number 8 on 21st March 1959) in the 1-0 home win versus Sheffield Wednesday. Alan scored some vital goals for the Millers in an ultimately successful battle against relegation. One of his most memorable matches came on 2nd September 1961 in the away match at Leeds United, when Rotherham United won 3-1 and Alan scored a great hat-trick. He eventually accumulated 144 League appearances for Rotherham United, scoring a creditable 58 times, and his last appearance was at centre forward on 7th September 1963 in the 1-3 away defeat at Swindon Town. He then moved on to Newcastle United, and recalls: "At the time I was on £20 a week at Millmoor. I remember getting on the train at Rotherham Masborough Station and travelling up to Newcastle for a meeting. The maximum wage was finished by then and they offered me a good pay rise, so I was happy to sign". He left Millers fans with fond memories of him notching the second goal in the first leg of the League Cup Final. [*Author's note*: When Alan scored two goals against Birmingham City on his debut for Manchester City, the third was an own-goal credited to Birmingham City's full back Jeff Hall, who played for England. Jeff Hall died of polio while still a professional footballer and his widely publicised death sparked a mass vaccination campaign. Barrie Dalby, of the Rotherham United Nostalgia Society, recalls being vaccinated on the Millmoor forecourt.]

Keith Bambridge (outside left)

Keith was a wing wizard whose dribbling skills, crossing ability, and a willingness to get stuck in endeared him to Millers fans. Keith Graham Bambridge was born in Parkgate on 1st September 1935 and attended Mexborough Grammar School where another pupil was Brian Sawyer with whom he was later to play in senior football. In his younger days, Keith was a keen supporter of Rotherham United and speaking at his home in February 2005 recalls: "At one match I was sitting on the wall at the edge of the pitch when I was hit hard by a ball kicked by Danny Williams. I fell backwards onto the old wooden railway sleepers which formed the terracing at that time, but I wasn't badly hurt." Out on the pitch he played for Mexborough Grammar School, and also for Don & Dearne Schoolboys as a winger. As a teenager he also played for the Ryecroft Methodist Youth Club (where he became friends with Brian Sawyer) but recalls his lucky break came when he was aged nineteen: "I had just signed for Masborough St Paul's of the Rotherham Premier League where I was spotted by a Rotherham United scout at a practice match. I signed a professional contract in February

1955, but it was on the understanding that I would be a part-timer, as it was my wish to continue with my career as a draughtsman." Keith was expected to train on two or three evenings a week, at Millmoor, with other part-timers, including Peter Perry. Keith initially made several appearances for the 'A' and Reserve teams and recalls: "Two people had a big influence on my early career, being Walter Brooks the trainer, and coach Dewiss Brown who was something of a mentor to me. Dewiss was an ex Stockport County and Rotherham United player, who was also a teacher at Wickersley School, and he was responsible for the United 'A' team. When I was playing for the 'A' team, and we were on coach trips to away games, Dewiss would make a point of having one-to-one sessions with players, talking through previous games and offering advice. He was a big help and influence for me. Dewiss later left England and set up a coaching school in Canada." [Dewiss Brown was Rotherham United's first officially appointed coach, joining the club in August 1950 as player-coach with responsibility for the juniors and reserves. Six members of the League Cup Final side were tutored by him in their younger days. He emigrated in 1959.] Keith made his first team debut on 14th September 1955 away at Barnsley and laughed as he recounted a fairly well-known story: "My mum and dad went along for the occasion and, when the team coach arrived at Oakwell, I went into the dressing rooms with the rest of the players. I got a pair of complimentary tickets, and popped outside to give them to mum and dad. But when I tried to get back into the ground, an official refused to believe I was a player and thought I was trying to get in for free. Eventually skipper Gladstone Guest came

In this classic picture from the late 1950s Keith Bambridge is shown in the Millers' black and white away strip, in action versus West Ham United. Keith is every inch the archetypal player of the period and shown wearing the style of boots which he talks about in Chapter 2. (Adrian Booth collection)

looking for me and got me back inside!" Keith became a fixture in the first team in that 1955/56 season, playing in 33 League games (scoring six goals) and two F.A. Cup matches, and his very first goal in League football was in that season's 2-1 home victory versus Nottingham Forest on 22nd October 1955. He retained his position in the first team in season 1956/57, but in 1957 was called up for his National Service: "I joined the Training Regiment of the Royal Corps of Signals, based at Catterick, but I was retained on a Rotherham United contract, and home-leave allowed me to make half a dozen appearances in 1957/58. I played for the Royal Corps of Signals on about ten occasions, where my team-mates included Jimmy Melia (later with Southampton), Gerry Young (of Sheffield Wednesday fame) and Stan Jones (of West Bromwich Albion)." With National Service completed, Keith returned to Rotherham United and from season 1958/59 was a regular performer, with one of his most fondly remembered moments coming on 3rd October 1959 at Bramall Lane: "The Blades were winning 2-0 at half-time but we made a great fight back in the second half and drew level. I scored in the 90th minute to clinch a famous 3-2 away win. Many years later I met a supporter who told me that I became his favourite player at that instant. Apparently he was so excited that the end of his rattle flew off and hit another supporter on the head!" After the drama of the League Cup Final, Keith's career with Rotherham United gradually fell into decline, brought about in part by various injuries. In 1961/62 Keith played only 14 League games, plus six cup-ties in which he scored one goal, whilst season 1962/63 saw just four League appearances, including his last game for the club, the 0-1 away defeat at Southampton on 11th May 1963. In this era he spent his time playing in the Reserves although this was not without its compensations as Rotherham United Reserves remained unbeaten in the North Regional League and won the championship, with Keith playing in – and captaining – most games. This triumph is also remembered by Barry Lyons who, speaking at his home in York on 20th January 2005 recalled: "I was a young trainee at the time, but still remember the great role that 'old pros' like Keith Bambridge played in that championship season. Those older players were a great help to the youngsters, advising and bringing us on, and giving us the benefit of their experience in training and out on the pitch." By 1963/64, Ian Butler had emerged as first-choice outside left with Keith having fallen out of favour at Millmoor and not featuring in the first team. It was clearly time for a parting of the ways. In his time at Rotherham United, Keith played a total of 162 League games (scoring 15 goals) and also represented the club in 17 cup matches (scoring one goal). He was never once booked, a fantastic record for a winger who was, on occasions, marked by fullbacks who were (to use Keith's own ironic term) 'somewhat physical'. Keith recalled that he tried to give fullbacks the impression that they were about to win the ball but, at the last second, he would attempt to whip the ball away and leave the defender stranded. This needed perfect timing and, if he was a bit out, Keith accepted that he would be kicked into the second row of the terracing! Another thing he had to put up with was opponents' elbows when they were chasing the ball together and recalls: "When Rotherham played Scunthorpe United in a drawn F.A. Cup tie, I was running past their outside right who elbowed me in the mouth and knocked out my two front teeth. After the match I was taken to a local dentist who made up a pallet and the denture was ready for the replay! A couple of years later I was talking to some fans and they told me they had been on the terraces exactly where the elbowing took place, and they retained a vivid image of me standing on the touchline spitting out teeth and blood." He never retaliated though and, with characteristic good humour, says: "if I *had* tried to give that outside right an elbowing back it would have inflicted a severe pain in his knee!" Talking of full backs, Keith recalls George Cohen, the England international, as being his most respected opponent and says: "The first time I played against him, I had a reasonable degree of success in the early part of the game, but later on found him a difficult proposition to get past."

Gordon Morritt was official twelfth man in the 2nd leg of the final at Villa Park. He is seen here in action against Leyton Orient in 1964/65, and the picture was signed by Gordon and Barry Lyons in April 2006. (Adrian Booth collection)

8. Players Who Appeared in Earlier Rounds

A grand total of sixteen players represented Rotherham United in the inaugural League Cup competition. In addition to the eleven who appeared in both legs of the final, a further five players appeared in the earlier rounds. These five were:

George Darwin
George scored in the away tie at Leicester City, his only appearance for Rotherham United in the League Cup competition. In fact the enigmatic George only played three games for the Millers, and his name is perhaps unfamiliar to many Rotherham supporters. Born at Chester le Street on 16th May 1932, Darwin started his professional career with Huddersfield Town where he was in the squad with Lol Morgan but, despite being with Town from 1950 to 1953, he failed to break into the first team. George gained his first League experience after transferring to Mansfield Town, for whom he made 126 League appearances and scored a highly respectable 63 goals between 1953 and 1957. His scoring feats attracted Derby County and, between 1957 and 1961, he played 94 League games for the Rams and scored 32 goals. George signed for Rotherham United in October 1960 (just before the Leicester City match) for a fee of £6,000, and had a spectacular opening to his Millmoor career. His first team debut came on 15th October 1960 in a 2-2 home match versus Huddersfield Town in which he scored, whilst on 22nd October 1960 away at Sunderland, he hit the Millers' goal in a 1-1 draw. His third game was the League Cup-tie away at Leicester City on 26th October 1960 and he scored yet again. In the Leicester City match programme it was noted: "In the team expected to be on duty here tonight, the most recent addition is inside forward George Darwin from Derby

George Darwin, who played one match and scored one goal for Rotherham United in the League Cup run. (Leicester Evening Mail)

County, a player who has drawn considerable attention at the Baseball Ground in the last few seasons." George made the amazing start of scoring three goals in three games in eleven days – and one cannot help but speculate that, if he had stayed for a few seasons and maintained anything like that ratio, he would have been a super hero! As mentioned in the Introduction, it has not proved possible to interview George Darwin but he is remembered with affection by Keith Bambridge who, speaking on 30th July 2005, said: "George Darwin was a fine player. He had played for Derby County against Rotherham United and, when the players heard that George was coming to Millmoor, they said how much they were looking forward to playing with him. He was a player who was held in high esteem by his fellow professionals for his great ball control skills and unselfish work. When he got injured so quickly in his Rotherham United career the players were sad to have lost a good team mate."

Brian Jackson
Brian played twice in the Millers' League Cup run, these games being the classic away victories at First Division Leicester City and Bolton Wanderers. He was born in Maltby on 2nd February 1936 and his first job upon leaving school was at Maltby Colliery. He grew up as a fine all-round sportsman and, whilst still in his teens, represented the Colliery at both cricket and football. Brian was a fine medium pace bowler and was invited to net practice for Yorkshire CCC at Headingley. Another famous cricketing Maltby-ite was Yorkshire and England fast bowling hero Fred Trueman, a family friend. Brian played for the Yorkshire CCC Second X1 along with team mates Ronnie Burnet, Jimmy Binks, Harold 'Dickie' Bird, Doug Padgett and Huddersfield Town's Ken Taylor (per Yorkshire CCC Yearbooks) and was twice selected as twelfth man for Yorkshire CCC First X1. Instead of cricket, however, he chose to be a professional footballer and, in September 1954, signed for Rotherham United as a part-time professional. Initially he was in the Millers' junior team which won the Northern Intermediate League

Brian Jackson and Danny Williams in Millers colours about 1959. Brian played two matches in the 1960/61 cup run but sadly is now deceased, while Danny went on to become a well known manager whose clubs included Rotherham United and Sheffield Wednesday. He was also in charge of Swindon Town when they beat Arsenal 3-1 in the 1969 League Cup final. (Graham Barnes collection)

championship in 1954/55, but made his first team League debut in season 1955/56 in the 3-2 home win versus West Ham United on 17th December 1955. Altogether that season he played ten games. In 1955 Brian commenced his National Service with the RAF in Lincolnshire, which restricted him to six appearances in 1956/57, three in 1957/58, just one in 1958/59, and six in 1959/60. Upon leaving the RAF he signed as a full time professional at Millmoor and is recalled as being a skilful half back with a precise accurate pass but, for all that, he never won a permanent place in the first team. In the cup final season of 1960/61 he played thirteen matches (including two cup ties), but 1963/64 was his best season by far, when he made 39 League appearances, although under trying circumstances. A knee injury sustained on a frosty pitch at Norwich City (on 23rd February 1963) caused him problems for a year but at that time he was important to the team and was allowed to do minimal training and just concentrate on playing in the matches. His last appearance for the club was at left half in the 1-0 home win versus Crystal Palace on 2nd January 1965. In his ten seasons at Millmoor, Brian clocked-up 131 League games and eleven cup appearances, notching six goals.

Keith Kettleborough

Keith was a hard working inside forward who played against Leicester City and Bristol Rovers in the League Cup run, and of whom Barry Webster said: "He was the best inside forward I ever played with". Keith was born in Rotherham on 29th June 1935 and was always a keen sportsman. Speaking at his home in Herringthorpe on 10th February 2005 Keith said: "As a teenager I grew up playing both cricket and football. If anything, I preferred cricket and played for Rotherham Boys, Yorkshire Boys, and the North of England Boys." As with most young men of his era, Keith had his spell of National Service (in the RAF), after which he returned to Rotherham and briefly worked in the steel industry. He recalled: "I did have a trial for Grimsby Town, but they did not sign me, and I probably could have gone into cricket on a professional basis, but in the event I chose professional football and joined Rotherham United." The July 1962 issue of *Charles Buchan's Football Monthly* records this in more detail, noting: "Keith Kettleborough might have become a Grimsby Town player. They spotted him when he was playing in R.A.F. football in Lincolnshire and invited him to have a fortnight's trial when his National Service ended. He played three matches in Grimsby's 'A' team, and took part in the practice games. Grimsby had doubts. They offered him another fortnight, but the uncertainty didn't suit Keith, so he went to his Rotherham home and took a job in the local steelworks. Rotherham United then signed him ..." Keith signed as a full time professional in December 1955, quickly making his first team debut at inside

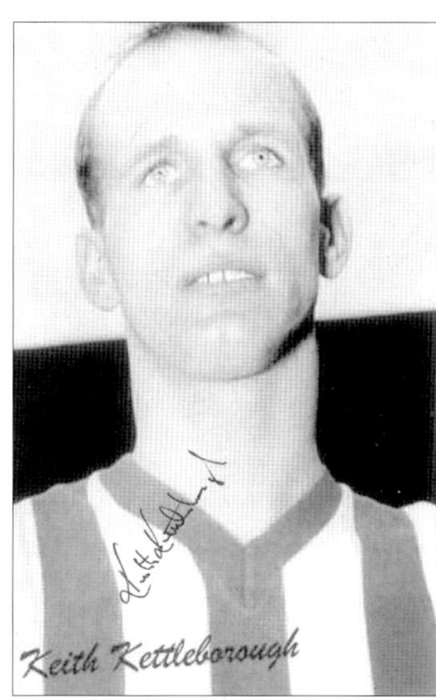

Keith Kettleborough has a permanent place in Rotherham United history by scoring the club's first ever goal in a League Cup match. He is shown here in Sheffield United colours, and signed the picture at his home on 10th February 2005. (Adrian Booth collection)

Eddie O'Hara, the Scottish winger who featured in one match during the Millers' run to the final. (Graham Barnes collection)

right in the F.A. Cup Third Round match versus Scunthorpe United on 7th January 1956. A period in the Reserves followed, and he made his first team League debut in the long haul away fixture at Plymouth Argyle on 14th April 1956, which was lost 1-3. In 1956/57 Keith made only a solitary appearance, coincidentally versus Sheffield United, but from 1957/58 was a regular in the first team. He represented Rotherham United until season 1960/61, playing his last game on 26th November 1960 in the 0-0 home draw versus Stoke City. Altogether Keith played 118 League games in which he scored 19 goals. His strike against Leicester City goes down in history as the first ever scored by a Millers player in the League Cup competition although, when speaking further on 10th February 2005, he did not realise he held this niche in Rotherham United's history. In fact Keith could not bring the goal to mind and joked: "It's funny that I can't remember that particular goal. I can remember all the others I scored in my career, as I didn't get that many!"

Eddie O'Hara

Scotsman Eddie played one game for the Millers in the famous cup run, versus Bristol Rovers on 23rd November 1960. Born in Glasgow on 28th October 1935, he began his career with Falkirk (1955 to 1958) for whom he played 95 Scottish League games and scored 18 goals. His big break came when Everton signed him in June 1958 and he played 29 League games (two goals) for the Toffeemen. He moved on to Rotherham United in February 1960 and made his first team debut on 27th February 1960 in the 1-1 draw away at Huddersfield Town. He played six consecutive games at number 11, before switching to play five matches at number 10, and notched goals against Stoke City and Lincoln City – the latter the only goal of the game. In 1960/61 he made a further nine League appearances, playing three times on the left wing and six games at number 10. After playing in the League Cup match, his last appearance for the club was three days later in a 0-0 home draw versus Stoke City, coincidentally also Keith Kettleborough's last match. What turned out to be Eddie's last goal for the club was scored in the 1-1 home draw versus Ipswich Town on 17th September 1960. Brian Sawyer recalls: "Eddie O'Hara was a Scot; a left winger and all left foot. He was not bad, but a bit on the slow side, and he did not play too often in the first team." Lol Morgan remembers: "Eddie married a Liverpool girl. He was a real character and, in fact, could be described as a bit of a rogue." Keith Bambridge noted: "I was always a part-time player at United and did my training in the evenings. At that time manager Tom Johnston was on the look out for a full-time left winger because obviously it was advantageous to have such a player at training sessions when corner kicks and left side free kick routines were being practised. The manager brought in Eddie O'Hara with a view to replacing me, but Tom obviously thought I had managed to fight-off his challenge for my first team slot!"

Brian Sawyer

Brian is remembered as being comfortably Rotherham United's fastest player of his era, once in full stride, and secondly for being unlucky at the start of season 1961/62 when a knee injury ruined his chance of playing in the League Cup Final. Born in Rawmarsh on 28th January 1938, Brian was an excellent all-round sportsman. Speaking at his home at Masham on 14th May 2005, Brian outlined his other skills (in addition to football) and also cleared up a couple of inaccuracies which have crept into other published references: "I first played football in the Mexborough Intermediate (under 18 league) for Ryecroft Methodists, when I was fourteen years of age. One of my team-mates at Ryecroft was Keith Bambridge but, when I played for Mexborough Grammar School (MGS), Keith was not in the same side, as is widely thought, as he is a couple of years older than me. I next played, in the same league, for Tom Hill Youth Club at Denaby in the 1954/55 season. I was one of half a dozen pals who left MGS at the same time and decided to join Tom Hill en-masse as a means of keeping playing together. We had a good side and 'walked' the league that year. I was seen by a scout from Barnsley FC and, aged 17, signed amateur forms for them, playing half a dozen games in their Junior side in the Northern Intermediate League. I actually played one game versus Rotherham United! Tim Ward, the Barnsley manager, wrote me a letter

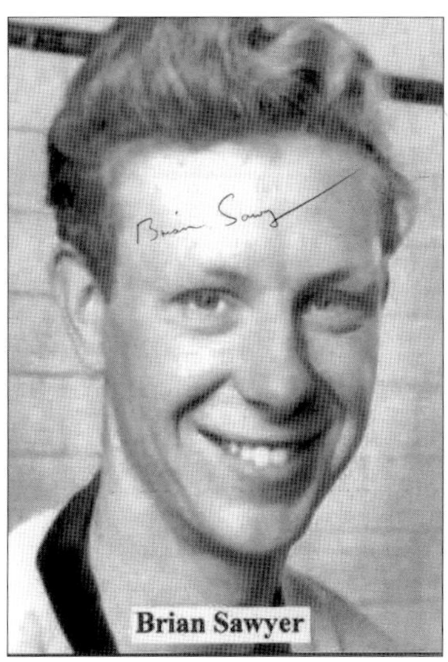

Rotherham's speedy striker Brian Sawyer, who played in five of the League Cup matches up to and including the semi finals, scoring two goals. When signing this photograph on 8th February 2005, Brian remarked that coincidentally it had been taken in the Villa Park dressing rooms on an earlier cup visit by the Millers. This was an F.A. Cup third round match played on 10th January 1959, in which Brian Sawyer scored in the Millers' 1-2 defeat before a crowd of 33,357. (Adrian Booth collection)

offering terms for 1955/56 as a junior, but I was unhappy at the way Barnsley ran their junior team. I talked it over with Keith Bambridge, who suggested playing for Rotherham United Juniors. Keith arranged for me to go to pre-season training and I signed amateur forms to play 1955/56 for Rotherham United in the Northern Intermediate League. I played half a season on the right wing but then David Layne came after Christmas. He was put on the right wing and I was switched to centre forward. I regarded myself as a right winger for my entire career and constantly switched from wing to wing when I was playing centre forward. I never played for Rawmarsh Welfare as has been widely reported." As with most young men in that era, Brian was called up for National Service and reported for duty with the RAF in August 1956 when aged 18. He was trained in radar and then posted to Jever in northern Germany, recalling: "When I got there, I discovered that the sports officer was a Rotherham man who was a Millers supporter and knew of me, and had pulled a few strings to get me into his section! It was in the RAF that I got into athletics and I competed for the Second Tactical Air Force (STAF) in Germany in both the 100 and 200 metres events, plus playing in the football team." At this time Brian also made his debut for the Rotherham United first team when still an amateur, in a definite case of 'wheels within wheels' as he recounted: "One day I got a message to report to the sports officer who told me that he had received a telephone call from the Millers manager, Andy Smailes. He said that there was a flu epidemic at Millmoor and asked if I could be released. They flew me across to Manchester, and then by car to Rotherham, where I made my debut on 4th January 1958 in the F.A. Cup third round versus Blackburn Rovers. For the first time in my life I played on the left wing, and we lost 1-4. I then flew back to Germany." Brian later made his League debut while at home on leave, on 7th April 1958 in a 1-5 home defeat to Charlton Athletic. He scored his first Millers goal in this game, recalling: "Albert Broadbent, the ex Sheffield Wednesday player, took a corner and I scored with a header. Andy Smailes managed to get my leave extended to play further games versus Bristol Rovers and Lincoln City. In the Lincoln game I scored a goal but the Referee disallowed it for 'ungentlemanly conduct' as I had pushed one of my own team mates out of the way! I then returned to Germany via Harwich and received an order by tannoy to report to the STAF team in Brussels, who were on a tour of Belgium and Holland. Papers and travelling passes were already prepared for me." After coming out of the RAF in August 1958, Brian signed professional for Rotherham United at £20 per week and £17 in the summer, but had to obtain special permission to complete in local tennis events, as professionals were then not allowed in amateur sport. He won the Mexborough & District tennis singles for three years running, as well as representing the Rotherham & District League. He played thirteen games for the Millers in 1958/59, but season 1959/60 was his best, finishing as the club's leading goal scorer with eighteen, including a run of netting in six successive games. Following surgery on his knee, which was injured on the close season tour of Finland prior to 1961/62 season, Brian's appearances for Rotherham United began to peter out. In 1962/63 he played in the Reserves and recalls one notable occasion: "We played an away match against Accrington Stanley Reserves at Peel Park and I played centre forward. Marking me that day was Neil Franklin, the well known former England international centre half." During 1962/63 he made a solitary, and last, first team appearance. This was on the right wing in the 2-2 away draw at Preston North End on 27th October 1962. Brian recalls: "It was just one of those days. I had a bad game. Later in the season Danny Williams called me into his office and I was introduced to the Bradford City manager. Following discussions, I accepted a transfer to Bradford City as part of the deal which brought John McCole to Rotherham United." Altogether Brian clocked up 90 League games plus 18 cup-ties for Rotherham United, scoring 31 League and 6 cup goals.

9. The Manager

The Rotherham United manager throughout the 1960/61 League Cup run was Tom Johnston. He arrived at Millmoor in December 1958 to replace Andy Smailes and his main brief was to stave off the threatened relegation to Division Three. He succeeded and thereafter led the Millers in a relatively successful period in Division Two. Tom was a Scotsman, being born on 30th December 1918 at Coldstream in the Border area. He was keen to break into professional football and was prepared to move away from the Borders area to achieve this, finding himself initially playing Midland League football for Peterborough United in 1939. While with the Posh he qualified as an F.A. Coach. He guested for Northampton Town and Leicester City during World War 2, and then played over fifty League games for Nottingham Forest after the end of hostilities. It is, however, with Notts County that he made his name as a player. The book *Notts County. The Official History 1862 – 1995* by Tony Brown (published 1996) reveals that Johnston played 267 League and 18 F.A. Cup games for the club between 1948 and 1956, scoring 88 and 4 goals respectively. He was never a full international but four times was reserve for Scotland before hanging up his boots. At the start of the 1957/58 season he was appointed as Youth Team coach at Birmingham City, whilst in January 1958 he became manager of Heanor Town, and was appointed at Millmoor in December 1958. Tom managed to save the club from relegation (finishing third from bottom), with an influential factor being his signing of goal scorer Alan Kirkman. He led Rotherham United in the great F.A. Cup victory over Arsenal, and of course was in charge for the 1960/61 League Cup run. Tom was also particularly successful in signing promising young players, and several who went on to great things first put pen to paper for Tom Johnston. Speaking on 28th April 2005, Brian Sawyer recalled: "Tom was certainly Scottish in his frugality. He cut us down on everything possible, training gear, boots, and travelling and did not worry too much about it making him unpopular. We all had to carry our own personal kit, and we almost had a strike once when Lol Morgan lost his boots on the way back from Ipswich Town. He insisted Lol or the other players paid for the replacements ourselves. In retrospect I suppose he was working to a strict budget and he certainly brought some much needed organisation to the club. He was also the first Rotherham United manager to my knowledge who was also a coach rather than a suit man. He tried numbers of things in training, but tended to get disheartened if they did not come off as he expected. One famous attempt by him to be totally in control backfired. When we drew the Brighton F.A. Cup replay he made us stay in Brighton, travel to Rotherham for the Cardiff game, pick up clothes from our wives and girlfriends under the Stand, and immediately go away again for a second replay. We were fed up and bored silly, and we all know what happened in the second replay. He was manipulative and a wheeler dealer, but in the end he did a good job of bringing the club forward." Taking up the coaching theme, when speaking on 23rd May 2005, Roy Lambert recalled: "Tom Johnston was a qualified coach. He could be a bit abrasive and some of the players did not get on with him very well. Tom used to get us practising

A portrait of manager Tom Johnston, taken from a Rotherham United Supporters Club publication. (Peter Perry collection)

new and different things in training. He would get us working on such as short corners, free kick routines, and getting players to make pre-planned dummy runs at throw ins and then throwing the ball into a space for a team mate to run on to." On 31st July 2005 Keith Bambridge said: "Tom Johnston was a good coach, but he knew how to manipulate people. I respected him as a football man, but I had loads of spats with him and I used to get lots of ribbing from the other players about how I used to rub Johnston up the wrong way. I remember on one occasion we played Leicester City and I came off the pitch at the end of the match, absolutely knackered, and feeling that I had played a particularly good game. Johnston just looked at me and said 'why don't you play like that every week?' That was typical of our relationship." Johnston left Rotherham United in August 1962 – being replaced as manager by Danny Williams – to take over at Grimsby Town, but is probably best remembered for his two separate spells in charge of Huddersfield Town, where published references described him as a 'strong disciplinarian' and being 'a dour and canny Scot'. He joined Huddersfield Town in season 1964/65, taking over from Eddie Boot and, referring to these two managers, the book *Huddersfield Town 75 Years On* notes: "Tom Johnston was of a similar mould; slightly more disciplined in his approach, but one who did not do much shouting yet was a shrewd strategist and expert judge of material." His periods at Huddersfield Town were either side of a long stint at York City, where he was in charge from 31st October 1968 to 11th January 1975. His 1974 York City side – which won promotion to Division Two – included Barry Lyons and Ian Butler, both of whom he originally signed as juniors whilst he was managing the Millers. After retiring from the game, Tom returned to live in Nottingham, where he was a keen golfer, but sadly he is now deceased.

The Rotherham United squad for season 1964/65. The rich crop of new youngsters are evident in this group, and the three remaining players from the 1960/61 final side – Lambert, Madden and Ironside – stand together at back left. (Rotherham United)

10. Where Did They Go?

Keith Bambridge
The player-manager at Darlington from the start of season 1964/65 was Lol Morgan, whilst Ken Waterhouse also moved to Feethams in August 1964. Lol had noted that Keith was languishing in Rotherham United Reserves and, in December 1964, came to Millmoor to see his former colleague and offer the chance to resurrect his League career in County Durham. Keith recalls: "Lol was the only left-footer in Darlington's first team, and he needed somebody else who could use his left peg. I made my debut for the Quakers on Boxing Day 1964 up at Hartlepool United, and the only way I could get there from Rotherham was by taxi. Fortunately at Darlington's expense! Shortly after I played in one of Darlington's biggest-ever games, when they took on Arsenal in the 3rd Round of the F.A. Cup, and I was marked by Don Howe. Unfortunately we lost 0-2." The match on 15th March 1965, at home to Stockport County, signalled the end of Keith's brief stay at Darlington and, after just seven matches, he was on his way. Things had not really worked out at Feethams, mainly due to travelling problems, particularly away games. Keith very quickly found a new club and, only five days after turning out for Darlington, he was back in his home county of Yorkshire and making his debut for Halifax Town. Keith remembers: "This came about because, after the Darlington v Stockport match, Lol Morgan told me that Halifax Town manager Willie Watson (the double international) was interested in signing me, wanting me to play at inside forward." As things turned out, Keith was to make just eight League appearances (plus one as substitute), and one League Cup appearance for Halifax Town. Sadly, Keith was destined never to play on the winning side for Halifax Town, the club losing nine and drawing just one of his ten appearances! Despite his short stay at the Shay, Keith holds a permanent place in the club's history on two counts. He is included on a Halifax Town team photograph taken prior to the first game of the 1965/66 season, versus Tranmere Rovers on 21st August 1965. This was the first day that substitutes were allowed in English League football, and then only one permitted in case of injury. Although not used in the Tranmere Rovers match, Keith was Halifax Town's first ever named substitute. In the away game versus Stockport County on 27th August 1965, he went on as substitute after 37 minutes – wearing the number 12 shirt – to replace Jeff Lee and so became the first ever substitute used by Halifax Town in a League match. In the game on 3rd September 1965 (coincidentally versus Darlington) he scored his only goal for Halifax Town, which was his very last in League football. His last-ever League game was versus Torquay United on 16th October 1965 when, coincidentally, his old Rotherham United team-mate Alan Kirkman was playing as a central defender for the Gulls. Keith had knee problems at this time, and recalls: "Halifax Town were very good to me and arranged an operation at Halifax General Hospital where both cartilages were removed from my right knee. I also went down to see a specialist in London, but was advised to retire from the professional game, so then I continued in my other career as a draughtsman." His knees may have been knackered as regards the rigours of professional football, but they were plenty good enough for the local scene, and Keith mesmerised many a fullback as he played on with (and coached) Dinnington, Rotherham Co-op, Centralians and Firth Brown's, until finally hanging up his boots for good in 1978, aged 43. He now lives in retirement at Bramley, and plays a round of golf whenever he can.

Keith Bambridge at his home in the Bramley area of Rotherham, on 3rd January 2005. (Adrian Booth)

George Darwin
After scoring three goals in three games for the Millers in October 1960, George's injury – sustained in the cup match away at Leicester City – finished his Millmoor playing career. He initially considered giving up the game but Ron Staniforth (with whom George had played at Huddersfield Town) was the manager of Barrow (who were then still a League club) and he persuaded George to give it

another go. Despite his bad knees, George was transferred to Barrow in July 1961, in the belief that his skill and experience would see him through at the lower level. Throughout his career he had a high goal per game ratio and continued in this vein for Barrow. In its issue dated 26th August 1961, the *Rotherham Advertiser* reported: "Inside forward George Darwin, transferred from Rotherham United to Barrow during the close season, scored twice – both penalty goals – for his new club in their 3-0 victory over Crewe Alexandra last Saturday. He scored again from the spot in Barrow's 1-0 win at Mansfield on Monday." In the Barrow v Accrington Stanley programme dated Monday 18th September 1961 (kick-off at 5-45pm), it recorded that Darwin had by then played his first six League games for Barrow and scored three goals. He is listed in the pen-pictures section of the Bradford City v Barrow programme dated 28th October 1961 where it is noted: "George Darwin (inside right) started his League career with Huddersfield and has played successively for Mansfield, Derby, Rotherham and Barrow, who paid their highest fee ever for him." George went on to play a total of 92 League games for Barrow (scoring 28 goals) before moving into non-league circles.

Ken Houghton

After two years of trying, Hull City finally snapped up their man in January 1965, at a reported fee of £45,000, also taking Houghton's team-mate Ian Butler within a week. Ken Houghton proved to be superb buy for City, playing alongside those famous team-mates Chris Chilton and Ken Wagstaff, as well as Ian Butler. He made his City debut on 9th January 1965 in a 3-2 away win at Bournemouth, and netted his first goal for the club on 6th February 1965 in a 3-1 home win versus Queens Park Rangers. Between 1964/65 and 1972/73 Ken made 290 (plus 14 as substitute) League and Cup appearances for the Tigers, netting 91 goals. The majority of his appearances were in the number 10 shirt, although he did occasionally wear other numbers. The book *Hull City, A Complete Record* (Breedon Books 1989) reveals Houghton to be the club's eighth highest all-time leading goal scorer, and one of only 27 players to have represented the club in over 250 League matches. Following his tremendous time at Hull City, he moved in June 1973 to Scunthorpe United, and season 1973/74 was his last as a League player. Speaking on 5th May 2005, Ken recalled: "I never wanted to leave Hull City, and my time at Scunthorpe United was not a happy period. What happened was that Hull City's manager, Terry Neill, was trying to sign Steve Deere from Scunthorpe United, but their manager Ron Ashman would not let him go unless I moved to Scunthorpe as part of the deal. So I reluctantly moved but, before I ever played, Ashman left and went to Grimsby Town. I never played a game for Ron Ashman! In those days the Humber Bridge had not been built, so I had to travel from my home in Hull and go via Goole for training and matches – and then all the way home again." Ken's first goal for Scunthorpe was on 1st September 1973 in the 3-0 home win versus Barnsley, and he was next on target on the 12th of that month in the amazing 2-7 away defeat at Gillingham. On the 29th he scored in the 1-1 home game versus Hartlepool United. Ken stuck out that one season at the Old Show Ground and then left. He was appointed player-manager of Scarborough FC in June 1974, where his philosophy of attacking football quickly made him very popular with the fans. He returned to his first club when in need of a new striker and, from Rotherham United, signed John Woodall at a then-record Scarborough transfer fee of £1,000. Woodall proved to be a wise investment, and went on to make 172 (plus 4 as substitute) appearances for Scarborough, scoring 76 goals. Houghton led by example out on

Ken Houghton at his home in the Anlaby area of Hull, on 13th January 2005. (Adrian Booth)

the pitch, appearing in over sixty games in 1974/75 (23 goals) and, at the end of the season, he proudly led out Scarborough at Wembley for the final of the F.A. Trophy. Played on 26th April 1975, the final versus Matlock Town proved a disaster, however, as the Seasiders lost 0-4. At the end of May 1975 the Scarborough Directors appointed former boss Colin Appleton (who had just been released by Grimsby Town) as general manager, whilst asking Houghton to remain in charge of team affairs. The alliance was doomed from the start and, saying that his position had been compromised, Houghton resigned on 20th June 1975. He moved twenty miles down the road, and had a short stay playing for Bridlington Town. In May 1976 Hull City invited Houghton to return to Boothferry Park as full time Youth Coach, a role which he grew to love. His great success in that position led to him being appointed Caretaker Manager in February 1978 upon the sacking of Bobby Collins, and Manager in April 1978. Two of Houghton's notable signings were Keith Edwards from Sheffield United and Trevor Phillips from Rotherham United, but inherited problems and inconsistency out on the park cost Houghton dear and his long association with Hull City ended with the sack in December 1979. Ken continued to live in Hull and worked for a local freight forwarding company, arranging the transporting of goods into Europe on behalf of British companies. For a while he played in local league football. Nowadays Ken lives in retirement with his wife at their home in Anlaby, at the west end of Hull. He still keenly follows the fortunes of Hull City and regularly attends their home games, along with his long-time pal Ken Wagstaff. Fans still remember him fondly and regularly chat to him about the old days, whilst from time to time he is asked to speak to local football organisations about his days with Hull City.

Roy Ironside was photographed on 9th June 2005 during a joint interview at Barry Webster's house at Jordanthorpe in Sheffield. He is seen holding Barry's tankard. (Adrian Booth)

Roy Ironside

Speaking on 9th June 2005, Roy said: "I signed in July 1965 for Barnsley, whose manager was then Johnny Steele and trainer Norman Rimmington, and I stayed there four years. Two of my playing colleagues in that era were the well known Eric Winstanley and former Millers junior George Hamstead." [Norman Rimmington was a former coal miner, and goalkeeper for Barnsley and Hartlepool United.] Roy was a member of the Barnsley team which won promotion from the Fourth Division in season 1967/68, finishing runners-up to Luton Town, and was a key member of the side which conceded 46 goals in 46 games. Altogether Roy played 113 League games for Barnsley and, when released, retired from football after a long professional career with just two clubs. Roy recalls: "At that time non league Worcester City tried to sign me. Their manager was Bill Jones, the former Cardiff City manager, and he had remembered me from when I had a good game when Rotherham United beat Cardiff City 4-1 away." [19th September 1959 before a crowd of 24,392] Barry Webster interjected: "Roy is just being modest there. At that time *The Sunday People* newspaper used to award players marks out of ten, and Roy played superbly that match and was given a rare 10 out of 10 rating!" Roy did not fancy moving down to Worcester, however, and started his own business, Sheffield Shopfitters, with a friend. The partnership lasted for many years until Roy went to work for Bedford & Havenhand Shopfitters, a company for who he still works, although these days on a part-time basis on the buying side. The famous Ironside name did not disappear from the League football scene after Roy's retirement, as he explains: "I have got four sons, and my second, Ian, was a keen footballer. In his younger days he was an outfield player, but I think he just had goalkeeping in his blood. He played initially for Matlock Town, but it was at North Ferriby United that Neil Warnock spotted him and signed him for Scarborough, which was then a League club. Ian went on to play League football for Scarborough (twice), Middlesbrough (in the top flight) and Stockport County." The football gene continues elsewhere in the Ironside family, and Roy says: "My youngest son Jamie is a goalkeeper and has just signed for Matlock Town. Looking to the future, Ian's own son Joe, now aged eleven, plays for Sheffield Boys and is at the Sheffield United Academy. He is a striker and natural goal scorer, and I have high hopes that he will make it in the game." Roy played cricket for 25 years for Sykes CC in the Norton & District League, although nowadays he suffers badly with arthritis in both knees and so keeps fit with regular workouts at his local gym. Roy recalls: "We had a great family atmosphere at Millmoor, all friends together, and all our wives knew each other" and he still looks back on his time at Rotherham United with affection.

Brian Jackson
Having not played for the first team since January 1965, Brian left Millmoor in July 1965 and made the short trip down the road to join Barnsley. He first played for Barnsley in season 1965/66, where he was appointed as club captain. Brian's stay at Oakwell was restricted to one season, however, when he played 29 games for the Tykes and did not register a goal. His knee injury had continued to trouble him and so he decided to retire from the professional game and went to work at Byford's Knitwear at Maltby, before returning to Maltby Colliery – as an onsetter – in 1978. His bad knee did not stop him playing cricket and he spent two seasons as professional with Upton in the Yorkshire Council. He later played for Maltby and Thurcroft before retiring from cricket in 1980, aged 44. Very sadly, Brian died several years ago. Returning from a holiday abroad with his wife, he was taken ill at the airport and admitted to hospital, but failed to recover. Speaking on 25th February 2005, Brian's former team-mate Roy Lambert paid him a lovely tribute: "Brian was quite a clever player on the ball, and very skilful. He was not a regular in the side, but whenever he came into the team he could be relied upon totally and never let you down. He was a good team man. He was also a very good cricketer and most people thought he was good enough to have played for Yorkshire. Several of we players attended his funeral and it was terribly sad – Brian wasn't very old. Most of all, I remember him as being a hell of a nice guy."

Keith Kettleborough
After playing in Rotherham's first two matches of the 1960/61 League Cup run, Keith was transferred to Sheffield United for a reported fee of £15,000. He played his first game for the Blades on 3rd December 1960 at home to Bristol Rovers in a Division Two match which United lost 2-3 (after being 2-0 up) before a crowd of 12,877. He almost made it to Wembley that year, as the Blades reached the semi final of the F.A. Cup, with

Keith Kettleborough at his home in the Herringthorpe area of Rotherham, on 10th February 2005. (Adrian Booth)

Keith in their line-up. They were paired against Leicester City at Elland Road, but the game was drawn, and it was only after two replays that City made it to the twin towers to meet Tottenham Hotspur. United's consolation was promotion to the First Division. Keith gave the Blades five years of excellent service (1960/61 to 1965/66) and was on the very fringe of full international honours. Altogether Keith played 154 League games for Sheffield United, scoring 17 goals. His last match was on 1st January 1966 at Bramall Lane in a Division One match versus Northampton Town, which was drawn 2-2 before 16,143 fans. In a surprise move, he then signed for Newcastle United at a fee of £22,500. The Newcastle United programme for the match versus Sheffield Wednesday on 5th February 1966 reported: "Of recent signing Keith Kettleborough, the *Mirror Sports* reporter had this to say – 'The Northerners star-turn was recent newcomer, inside left Keith Kettleborough, a study of perpetual motion, pin-pointing long defence splitting passes with astonishing accuracy. Kettleborough is certainly streets ahead of many who have worn England's colours this season.' That was praise indeed, and should delight supporters and those who negotiated the deal that brought him to St James' Park. Kettleborough, it should be noted, has not been on the losing side since manager Mr Joe Harvey signed him from Sheffield United four matches ago." It was ironic that the sports reporter should mention Keith's England credentials for, speaking of that era at his home on 31st August 2004, he recalled: "In 1963 I played for the Football League versus the League of Ireland, and was called-up for the England squad for several full internationals in 1965, being fully involved in the build-up training sessions. Unfortunately, no substitutes were allowed in that era. There was no making half a dozen substitutions at half time, and no getting a cheap full cap by going on to play the last two minutes of a game. In those days, if you did not make it into the final eleven for the match, you just had to sit in the stand and watch. I was also named by Alf Ramsey in his initial squad for the 1966 World Cup. I worked hard but, when Ramsey trimmed his squad down to the required 22 players, my name was unfortunately not on the list." Keith never did win that elusive full cap, and unfortunately never really settled on Tyneside. His stay with Newcastle United was a short one and he played just thirty games without scoring. In December 1966 he was pleased to move back to his South Yorkshire homeland, having signed for Doncaster Rovers for £12,000 as their player-manager. His first match was on 17th December 1966 at home to Peterborough United, a game that Rovers won 3-1 with an Alick Jeffrey hat-trick. Altogether that season Keith played 22 games (no goals) for the Rovers, although at the end of 1966/67 he was given the sack as manager. He was retained as a player and in 1967/68 played 13 League games plus one in the cup (no goals) before being transferred in November 1967 to Chesterfield for a fee of £6,000. He played a total of 66 League games for the Spireites (three goals) before moving into the non-league scene with Matlock Town. Speaking at his home on 10th February 2005 Keith said: "By this time my wife and myself had moved into a newly built house in Herringthorpe, Rotherham, and I was self-employed having purchased a local milk round. For about twenty years I worked on this round, until I sold-up as the business slowly declined due to customers gradually moving to purchasing their milk from supermarkets. I then worked as Clerk of Works at Birkdale Preparatory School in Sheffield where, besides looking after the buildings, I fitted in coaching cricket and football to the youngsters. I continued to play cricket, long after retiring from football, and played for Rotherham Town in the Yorkshire League, Rawmarsh, and Whiston Parish Church. I also played for The Stag pub side in local cup competitions, with the side also featuring Charlie Lee, the former Derbyshire CCC captain, who also lived in Herringthorpe. These days I am retired, but am kept fully occupied in helping to look after my grandchildren, plus fitting in regular rounds of golf at the Sitwell Park course. We still live in the same house, with a lovely set of friendly neighbours, many of whom also moved into their properties when newly built." [*author's note*: my late dad was a friend of Keith Kettleborough and one of my early football memories is going to watch Sheffield United away at Manchester City on 31st March 1962, and feeling very proud when Keith emerged from the Player's Entrance to give us a pair of complimentary stand tickets. I have still got my ticket. Keith signed a couple of autographs for City fans while we stood chatting. In the 1970s Keith delivered milk to our house and it always seemed strange when a former Millers and Blades hero knocked on our door each week to be paid!]

Alan Kirkman

Alan left Rotherham United in September 1963 and, like his old team-mate Keith Kettleborough, moved to Newcastle United – for a fee of £12,000. Like Keith, his stay on Tyneside was brief.

Alan Kirkman at his home at Horwich, near Bolton, on 11th March 2005. (Adrian Booth)

Speaking on 11th March 2005 Alan recalled: "Joe Harvey, the Newcastle United manager [born at New Edlington between Conisbrough and Doncaster] came in for me, and he was a really nice man. The fans were absolutely fantastic but I never settled on Tyneside. I only played five League games for the Magpies, scoring one goal, but a knee injury put paid to my first team spot and I felt that it was already time I was on my way." Alan moved in December 1963 to sign for Scunthorpe United, who were then still playing at the Old Show Ground. The Iron's manager was the former Leeds United player Freddie Goodwin, and Alan went on to play 32 League games (scoring five goals) as an inside forward up to the end of season 1964/65. He left the Old Show Ground after the Torquay United manager, Frank O'Farrell, went up to Scunthorpe to speak to Alan, explaining he wanted him to bring some experience to his team. Alan signed for Torquay United and was initially used by them up front, although he was later employed in a 'sweeper' role. The move certainly paid off, with Torquay United winning promotion from the old Fourth Division that season (1965/66) with 58 points, only one less than champions Doncaster Rovers. That season led to an unusual encounter between two old team mates. Keith Bambridge played his own last-ever League match (for Halifax Town) against Torquay United on 16th October 1965. Speaking on 10th February 2005, Keith recalled: "It was a strange thing that, in my last match, I came up against Alan Kirkman who Torquay were using as a defender, where his great experience was valuable to them. Funnily enough, with me being out on the wing, and Alan mostly in the middle, our paths hardly crossed and I can remember very few tackles between us". After clocking-up 59 League games for the Gulls (scoring eight goals) Kirkman moved from Devon way up to the Cumbrian coast and in January 1967 signed for Workington FC, an outfit that was a League club from season 1951/52 to 1976/77. The club was correctly Workington FC although they were widely known as 'Workington Reds'. Many opposition clubs put 'Workington Town' on programme covers, but this was in error, as Town are Workington's rugby league club. Alan explains the reason for this unusual move: "At the time Workington Reds were managed by Bill Leivers, who was a former colleague of mine at Manchester City and he signed me for my experience". His debut for the Reds was on Saturday 28th January 1967, playing at number 10 in the home game versus Colchester United. The match programme reveals that Workington had experienced an awful run of results over the previous few months and, in his column, Bill Leivers wrote: "Today we welcome our new inside forward Alan Kirkman, a player for whom I have the greatest admiration. I am sure he will be a great asset to us in our bid to stave off relegation. It is rather unique that within a fortnight we have signed two inside forwards from the same club. Tommy Spratt joined us from Torquay and now Alan has followed him north." Alan did indeed help Workington's fight, and it would be another ten years before the club lost its League status. Alan played 56 League games for Workington (scoring three goals) up to the end of season 1967/68, at which time he left the full-time game. Like Keith Bambridge, he had the fantastic record of never once being booked throughout his entire professional career. He moved back to live in Bolton in 1968 and there got a job with Hargreaves Transport, a company with which he stayed until his retirement. At the start of 1968/69 he moved into the non-league scene and spent two seasons as player-manager of Netherfield (a club based at Kendal in the Lake District) in the newly formed Northern Premier League. Macclesfield Town, Northwich Victoria and Wigan Athletic were numbered amongst Netherfield's opponents in those days. From season 1970/71 he was player-manager of Rossendale in the Cheshire League and, when they won the championship, Alan was voted Manager of the Year. In 1972 he broke his leg, which finished him as a player, although he continued for a while as manager only. The owner of his employer, Hargreaves Transport, was also Chairman of Horwich RMI football club and, from season 1972/73, Alan began a sixteen year spell as manager of Horwich RMI, initially in the Cheshire League. These days Alan lives in retirement at Horwich, and is still keenly interested in the semi-professional game, being a regular spectator at Leigh RMI, Atherton and Chorley, and occasionally taking in big games at Bolton Wanderers.

Roy Lambert

Roy made his last first team appearance for the Millers in April 1965 and, such is the esteem in which he is still held, that many fans have possibly forgotten that Roy briefly played for local rivals Barnsley. Speaking at his home in Swinton on 10th June 2005, Roy recalled: "I signed-on at Oakwell when they were a Fourth Division club, and Johnny Steele was manager and Norman Rimmington the trainer. Roy Ironside was already there. I played my first Barnsley game in November 1965, but I only played three games for them, two in the League plus one cup-tie. I also played in an away match at Southport which was abandoned due to fog, and so this did not count towards my total."

Roy Lambert at his home at Swinton, on 10th June 2005. (Adrian Booth)

The cup-tie was significant for Roy as it was his last ever game as a professional. He remembers: "It was a 2nd Round F.A. Cup match at home to Grimsby Town [on Saturday 4th December 1965] and we drew 1-1 with George Kerr scoring the Barnsley goal. In those days cup replays were played the following mid-week, so Johnny Steele had us in for training on the Sunday. During that training session I was turning after the ball and felt something 'go' in my back, and I was taken to Barnsley Beckett Hospital. I was diagnosed with a spinal injury and put in a 'pot jacket' followed by a couple of weeks convalescing at a small hospital near Ingbirchworth. I never played again and was out of football for a year." It was his old manager at Rotherham United, Tom Johnston, who got Roy back into the game. In 1966 Tom was manager of Huddersfield Town and he offered Roy a position of Youth Team Coach. Roy takes up the story: "I had my doubts at first because I was not qualified as a coach, but Tom said he would send me on the required courses down at Lilleshall. [A major sports centre opened in 1950 a couple of miles to the north-east of Telford in Shropshire.] I took the job with Huddersfield Town and qualified as a full F.A. coach. Tom Johnston then left [to take over as manager of York City in October 1968] and was replaced as manager by Ian Greaves, who called me into his office and told me he was also making me Chief Scout." It was a fantastic period at Huddersfield Town under Ian Greaves, with the side promoted to the First Division at the end of 1969/70 and with stars such as Trevor Cherry and Frank Worthington. They were in the top flight until relegated at the end of 1971/72. Meanwhile, the youth team got to the final of the F.A. Youth Cup in 1973/74, for the first time in the club's history and Roy recalls: "The final was a two-leg match versus Tottenham Hotspur. The away leg at White Hart Lane finished 1-1 and so the second leg created fantastic interest in Huddersfield [played on Tuesday 14th May 1974 and attracting a crowd of 15,300] although we lost that game 0-1 after extra time." Unfortunately, after Town were relegated from the top flight, they went into free-fall and at the end of 1974/75 were relegated into the Fourth Division. Ian Greaves left, and Tom Johnston was reappointed in difficult circumstances. Roy remembers: "Money was tight then and, strangely, it was Tom Johnston who had the task of telling me that I was sacked. I then gave up full-time football and took a job at Gerrard's at Kilnhurst and worked there for fifteen years until I retired in 1990 after being made redundant." Although giving up the full time game, Roy nevertheless kept involved in the professional game, via a couple of old contacts: "During my time at Gerrard's I did some scouting for Bolton Wanderers when Ian Greaves was manager. One thing which Ian liked me to do was to go to watch teams who Bolton were about to play, and then produce reports for him on their tactics and all the players. I also did some scouting for Burnley when Frank Casper was their manager." These days Roy lives in retirement with his wife Mavis in a gorgeous 300 year old cottage at Swinton, which has a lovely cottage garden. He still suffers pain from his old spinal injury, but retains a great love for the Millers and is practically an ever-present at the monthly meetings of the Rotherham United Nostalgia Society.

Peter Madden

In the match programme for the Rotherham United versus S.C. Telstar (Holland) friendly match played on Monday 2nd May 1966, there was a tribute to Peter Madden. Under a heading 'Peter Madden – Good and Faithful Servant' it was reported: "It has been officially announced that the club is to give a 'free' transfer to Peter Madden, our captain for several of his more than ten years. This marks the end of a distinguished Millmoor career for Peter, who has played 351 League and Cup matches, plus numerous other games. In a club where long-service records are not uncommon, the games total is not unique. It is, however, a tremendous achievement and a credit to the holder. Everyone at Millmoor wishes Peter the utmost success and happiness in the days ahead. The giving of a 'free' transfer invariably makes it much easier for players to join other clubs, where perhaps resources are limited. The club is happy to give Peter what help it can." [Peter Madden actually made 353 appearances for United, including two as a substitute.] Utilising his free transfer status, Peter moved back to his home town and, in July 1966, signed-on for Bradford Park Avenue who, in those days, were still a League club. Speaking at his home on 11th March 2005 Peter recalled: "The manager who signed me was Jock Buchanan, and Bobby Ham (later at Rotherham United) and Kevin Hector were team mates. I was captain there for a while." He played 28 League games for Park Avenue and scored one goal. Peter Madden finished his League career 'down south' after a seemingly surprising move to Aldershot in July 1967. Peter explains: "that move came about because Aldershot's manager at that time was Tom McAnearney, who I knew well from his time at Sheffield Wednesday. Tom was seeking an experienced centre half and contacted me to see if I was interested in the move. He made me his captain." Peter clocked-up a further 27 League games in season 1967/68 and scored his last-ever League goal. He comments: "I can picture that last goal – it was a header in a home game – but I cannot remember who it was against. [AFS records show Peter's last goal was Aldershot's first in a 3-1 home win against Wrexham on Saturday 21st October 1967. At the time Aldershot were second in Division 4 but fell away to finish ninth.] My time at Aldershot finished a bit earlier than I expected. I suffered a bad training injury when I accidentally kicked the goal post

Peter Madden at his home at Smithy Bridge, near Rochdale, on 11th March 2005. (Adrian Booth)

when attempting to clear the ball, and this damaged my ankle and caused damage further up my leg. That injury finished my professional career although I owe a debt of gratitude to Aldershot's physiotherapist who worked hard on my leg." He then moved back north to drift into the non-league scene as player-manager of Skegness Town with effect from August 1968. Peter remembers: "Skegness came in for me as they wanted an experienced player-manager. The match I recall best is a Lincolnshire Cup match against Scunthorpe United when both Kevin Keegan and Ray Clemence were in the Iron's line-up." Having gained two year's experience of management, Peter returned to the League scene as trainer-coach of Rochdale (August 1970), assistant-manager to Dick Connor at Darlington (August 1975), and was later promoted to manager at Feethams. After a disagreement with the Board, he resigned and returned to Rochdale as assistant-manager to Dougie Collins in October 1978. Peter took over as Rochdale manager in summer 1980 when Bob Stokoe left commenting: "They don't need a man, they need God!" Peter outlined his philosophy: "Even when I was a little kid I was always a winner and needed to win whatever I was playing. During my playing career I tried to learn from every manager I played under, and when they did something I did not agree with, I remembered it and later tried never to do that myself. As a manager, I tried my best to be firm but fair. I always wanted 100 per cent players – winners – in my sides. If ever we had any problems in the squad I always got things out in the open so we could discuss things freely, all say our piece, and then get on with it like men." Peter stayed at Rochdale until March 1983 but then gave up the professional game and became a turf accountant, before entering the licensed trade. In early 1985 he took over Topham's Tavern at Smithy Bridge (on the outskirts of Rochdale), a pub that had a team in the 4th Division of the Rochdale Sunday League. He became player-coach of the pub team and, upon his appointment, made them start training. The players initially complained: "Surely we don't have to train for Sunday League games?" to which Peter responded: "You do if I'm in charge!" The training paid off and Peter recalls: "I was at centre half, and the team were promoted from the 4th Division to the Premier Division in successive seasons. My last competitive game was when I was aged 57. The match was a 2-2 draw and I scored the equalising goal with a header. It was practically the end of the 1991/92 season and I thought it was a nice moment to bow out of playing. After that I was just team manager." Peter gave up the pub in 2000, but still lives at Smithy Bridge, now in retirement, with his wife Christine. These days he rarely goes to watch football, preferring his lifelong interest in horse racing, and also meets his pal two or three times a week for a game of snooker.

Lol Morgan

After ten years and 326 games for Rotherham United, Lol's place at left back was being firmly challenged by Colin Clish, whom Rotherham had signed from Newcastle United. Thus, when Lol saw a newspaper advert from Darlington FC, who were seeking a manager, he put in his application. Speaking at his home on 14th April 2005 he recalled: "By that time I was a qualified coach, having done the F.A. courses at Lilleshall with Brian Sawyer. I went up to Darlington for an interview [in June 1964] and was offered the position of player-manager on a

Lol Morgan at his home off Moorgate, Rotherham, on 14th April 2005. (Adrian Booth)

wage of £30 per week plus £4 win and £2 draw bonus. I started there just prior to the start of season 1964/65 and moved my family to live in Darlington. I was really short of players when I got there, and soon signed Joe Jacques from Lincoln City and Ken Waterhouse, who was then with Bristol City. Unfortunately it did not work out for Ken, as he was a very refined player whose game was not really suited to the hurly burly of the Fourth Division, and I used him in the Reserves to help with younger players. I also signed Keith Bambridge, but he left after half a dozen games because of travelling difficulties." Lol soon made a success of the job at Darlington, gaining promotion in his second year, but left in unfortunate circumstances. He recalls: "I really enjoyed my time at Darlington. We had a good team spirit, some good lads and no superstars to spoil things. I would have been happy to stay but, after promotion was won, the Chairman offered me a £5 per week pay rise which I was not happy with. I was a free agent in July 1966 and Norwich City got wind of my situation and arrangements were made for me to meet their Secretary at Doncaster. They offered me the job – as Manager only – on a two year contract, and I succeeded Ron Ashman at Carrow Road ready for the start of the 1966/67 season. I again moved my wife and kids to a new house in Norwich." [Lol played 29 League games, plus one as substitute for Darlington.] In the event Lol gained a contract extension and stayed almost three years at Norwich City. He takes up the story, recalling: "I got the sack towards the end of the 1968/69 season after Derby County beat us fairly easily in a mid-week match at Carrow Road. [Norwich City 1, Derby County 4, on Wednesday 16th April 1969.] I was not actually at the game, being away on a scouting mission, but I received a telephone call telling me to report to the Chairman's office on Thursday morning. That was the end of my association with Norwich City!" Lol then moved his family back to Rotherham, where they got a house on Dovedale Road in Herringthorpe. He received an approach from Darlington FC, who were interested in having him back, but the proposal foundered when Lol was not willing to move his family home again, whilst Darlington insisted on their manager living in the town. Lol took a job (out of football, and which he hated) as Organisation & Methods Officer at Arthur Lee's. Around this time Lol went along as a spectator to watch Sheffield Wednesday versus Tottenham Hotspur and this fortuitously led to an interesting meeting: "I was in the corridor at Hillsborough and bumped into the Spurs manager Bill Nicholson. We got chatting, and I told him I was presently out of the game. One thing led to another, and I got the job as the Northern Scout for Spurs which I did for two or three years." Lol could have had other jobs in this era: "The Bradford City Chairman offered me the job as manager, and Bobby Robson at Ipswich Town offered me the job as his Chief Scout, but I turned them both down as I did not want to uproot my family yet again." Lol left the professional game in 1972 when he saw an advert in the *Sheffield Star* from Bass Brewery who were seeking a free trade representative. He got the job and, including various promotions, thoroughly enjoyed his twenty years with Bass. Lol kept himself fit by playing at Rotherham Golf Club, where he is a member to this day. Lol and his wife now live in retirement in their home off Moorgate, Rotherham.

Scotland Under 23 international Eddie O'Hara played at outside left for Greenock Morton in a friendly match at Barnsley, on Wednesday 14th February 1962.This is the cover of the match programme. Eddie signed for the Oakwell club in July 1962 and, although it is purely conjecture, it seems likely that his performance in the friendly game was remembered by the Barnsley manager and led to his transfer. (Adrian Booth collection)

Eddie O'Hara

Eddie's 21 spasmodic appearances in the Millers' first team came to an end in 1960/61, when he moved back to Scotland to play for Greenock Morton. After 29 Scottish League appearances (five goals) he returned to South Yorkshire and signed for Barnsley in July 1962. He was still with Barnsley in 1963/64 and played at outside left when the Tykes took on Manchester United at Oakwell in the F.A. Cup 5th Round on 15th February 1964. That day the United line up included Law, Best and Charlton, whilst O'Hara was marked by right back Seamus Brennan. The book *The Definitive Barnsley* records that Eddie last played for the Tykes in 1964/65 and altogether represented the club in 127 League, and 20 F.A. and F.L. Cup matches, scoring 37 and 4 goals respectively, before emigrating to South Africa where he signed for Bloemfontein City. There the trail runs cold. None of his former Rotherham United team mates are still in contact with Eddie

Peter Perry at his home in the Handsworth area of Sheffield, on 15th April 2005. (Adrian Booth)

and, in the absence of any up to date information, it remains a possibility that he may still be living in South Africa.

Peter Perry

Peter left Millmoor one agonising game short of clocking up a century of League appearances, although he did play well over one hundred games including cup matches. He signed-on with York City, whose manager was then Tom Lockie, for season 1962/63. The book *York City, A Complete Record* (Breedon Books) reveals Peter made his debut for the Minstermen on 22nd September 1962 in a dramatic 3-4 home defeat to Chesterfield. He had made only four first team appearances by the beginning of March 1963, of which three games were at right back and one on the left, but he then won the No.3 place. Starting on 11th March versus Darlington (away) he made nineteen consecutive appearances at left back. Peter was not the City penalty taker and his 23 League appearances in that campaign brought no goals. He was asked on 15th April 2005 about the arrangements involved in playing for the Minstermen, and replied: "When I was with York City I was still living at Treeton and working at Orgreave Coking Plant, so arrangements were made for me to do my training in the evenings with Rotherham United Reserves. On match days I went on the No.132 bus from Treeton to Rotherham and then caught a train from Rotherham to York. I used to meet up with Peter Wragg, another former Rotherham United player, who was also with York City at that time. The main problem was a York City club rule that required all players to report to the ground for away matches, and exceptions were not allowed, whatever the circumstances. I remember on one occasion we were away at Brentford and I had to get up out of bed at 5am and was off out of the house at 6am. I travelled on the train up to York, walked from the station to the ground, and eventually we set off for Brentford. We passed back through Rotherham about 10am!" [The fixture was Brentford versus York City on Easter Monday, 15th April 1963, kick off 3-15pm, which the home side won 2-1. The crowd of 15,070 was the biggest that City played before that season in any competition.] Peter names Jackie Fountain and Walter Gould, both ex Sheffield United, as other team mates. [Fountain was an 'ever present' that season.] The travelling was a bit of a problem so at the end of the season Peter and York City had a parting of the ways and, from season 1963/64, he bowed out of League soccer. Peter was never once booked throughout his League career. He signed for Gainsborough Trinity whose manager was Gladstone Guest and they played in the Midland League. Peter recalls: "After a couple of seasons at Trinity, I had one season at Goole Town who were also in the Midland League. After that my knees were beginning to play-up a little, so I dropped levels and had a period with Thorne Colliery in Yorkshire League Division One. We had a good side, also including Barry Webster, but I finished my playing career there because of bad knees." Outside the game, Peter always enjoyed cricket, and played for the Orgreave Works side aged into his fifties. He was a fast bowler, but also recalls once hitting 98 runs, his best ever score with the bat. These days he lives in retirement, with his wife Anne, in the Handsworth district of Sheffield. His main interests are gardening and taking regular holidays in Cyprus and Malta. He is rarely seen at football matches, just occasionally going to Hillsborough with his son who is a keen Wednesdayite.

Brian Sawyer

Brian was transferred to Bradford City in December 1962 as part of the John McCole deal, and played 15 games for City, including a cup tie versus Newcastle United, scoring two goals. Speaking on 14th May 2005 he recalled: "At this time Barry Webster was also playing for City. He had just bought a car and we used to travel together to Bradford each day for training, and also for matches. Barry and

Brian Sawyer at his home at Masham in North Yorkshire, on 14th May 2005. (Adrian Booth)

I were both released at the end of the 1963/64 season." Brian then dropped into the non-league semi-professional scene with Buxton, whose manager was Norman Curtis the former Sheffield Wednesday player, and played one season there in the Cheshire League. He then moved to Worksop Town, where they won the Midland League championship in 1965/66, his first season. After several happy years at Worksop Town he played as an amateur for Frickley Colliery. He then had three seasons at Skegness Town before hanging up his boots at the end of season 1974/75. His knee was less of a problem in the non-league game where he had the skill to cope, although he did have a further operation while at Skegness Town. Thereafter he just played in a few charity matches, plus games at prisons, for a local side colloquially known as the 'Ale Carts' with Keith Bambridge and Keith Kettleborough as team mates. While playing in non-league football, Brian's jobs were as an Advertising Salesman with Sheffield Newspapers, followed by a Free Trade Representative for Bass Mitchell & Butler. Brian also recalled: "Whilst at Millmoor I got my preliminary coaching badge in 1961/62 and in the summer of 1962 attended Lilleshall with Lol Morgan and got my full F.A. coaching badge when aged only 24. When I was in the non-league game I was able to use my qualifications and did paid part-time work for the Football Association, coaching in evenings and at weekends at boys clubs and youth clubs, etc, around the Rotherham area. In the summer of 1968 I was due to go coaching to Zambia with the F.A. but, playing for Worksop Town versus Retford Town on 13th April 1968, I got kicked in the stomach and burst my intestine, so could not go. While lying in my hospital bed I decided to change direction in my life and gave up coaching. I qualified as a teacher, with English as my main subject." After a few years in teaching Brian changed direction again: "I got a job with Globe Petroleum, operating out of Scunthorpe, and rose to be Retail Manager, buying and pricing petrol. We were taken over by Conoco in 1980, and I stayed with them until 1994 when I was able to take an early retirement package, aged 56." Besides football, Brian continued with other sports in his younger days and recalls: "I won cups, medals, shields, etc, at athletics, tennis, golf, and even bowls, but these trophies are all now stored somewhere in the garage. It's all a long time in the past now. I did not take up golf until well after I finished professional football, in my mid-40s actually, but it is the one game I cannot play as well as I would like and have never been better than an eleven handicap. Fly fishing has been my real passion throughout my life. I fish for trout, and have fly fished in Alaska, Norway, twice in Russia, as well as a trip for the big trout of New Zealand. Fly fishing is even the reason why we moved to live at Masham in North Yorkshire!" Nowadays Brian lives in retirement in Masham, with his wife Dorothy, where fishing, golf and walking occupy his days. He passionately watches football on television but never attends live games.

Ken Waterhouse at his home near Lancaster, on 11th March 2005. (Adrian Booth)

Ken Waterhouse

When released by Rotherham United, Ken moved to the south-west and signed on 5th April 1963 for Bristol City. Speaking at his home on 11th March 2005 Ken recalled: "At the time Bristol City were a struggling club and their manager Fred Ford approached me to bring in a bit of experience. My wife Dorothy and myself had been very happy living in Rotherham, and I had enjoyed my time with United, but we decided to move home to Bristol." Ken was at Ashton Gate for sixteen months and made sixteen League appearances in which he scored once. The goal, which proved to be his last in first-class football, was versus Bristol Rovers at Ashton Gate on Tuesday 23rd April 1963. City won 4-1 in front of 22,739 fans, and Ken hit the fourth goal. At the end of 1963/64 Ken was released and for a while there was a possibility of him going non-league and signing for Weymouth. However, he was transferred to Darlington where former Rotherham United colleague Lol Morgan had taken over as player-manager from the beginning of season 1964/65. In August 1964 Ken and Dorothy moved house again! Lol utilised Ken to bring his experience to bear by bringing-on the club's reserves. He actually played a solitary first team match for Darlington, however, which was his last first class game, and recalls: "My one game in the first team was versus Bury at Gigg Lane and Colin Bell was playing against us, but basically I played a full season in the reserves." [The game was Bury v Darlington on 23rd September 1964 in the 2nd round of the Football League Cup. Ken played right half, and Bury won 1-0.] Ken continued: "I recall that Darlington played Arsenal in the F.A. Cup 3rd Round [Arsenal won 2-0.] and I was present at the ground on that big day. When the season was over I left Darlington and, as a very temporary measure, got a job as a car salesman at a garage at Kendal. We almost moved back to Southport, but I saw an advert in the *Daily Express* newspaper where Morecambe FC was seeking a full time player-manager. I had played several times at Morecambe in my younger days for Preston North End, in friendly matches, and I quite fancied the job, particularly as it was in my native north-west coast area. I applied for the job and I think my Preston North End connections probably helped in me being offered the position, so we were soon moving house again, leaving Darlington and moving into a Morecambe FC club house. I was later told that my chief rival for the job was none other than Brian Clough! I began my new career with Morecambe in the 1965/66 season in the Lancashire Combination, and we won the championship in 1966/67 and 1967/68 while I was in charge. We also won the League Cup in 1967 and 1968 and the Lancashire Senior Cup in 1968 beating Burnley 2-1 in the final. I played for Morecambe until October 1967 when, in a game versus St Helens Town, one of their players broke my leg with an appalling crude tackle." Ken stayed on as manager until 1969, but Morecambe really wanted a player-manager so it was time for him to go. [At Morecambe, Ken played 76 league games scoring 2 goals, plus 33 cup-ties with a single goal.] Ken continued his story by recalling: "We moved out of the Morecambe FC club house into a property of our own in the town. I had got my full F.A. coaching badges after attending all the required courses at Lilleshall, and Blackburn Rovers came in for me and offered a job as reserve team coach at Ewood Park. I travelled every day for eighteen months from Morecambe to Blackburn and back by car. I then had a chance to join Harry Catterick, who offered me a position at Everton, but I turned it down and actually rejoined Morecambe FC as manager in season 1971/72. The former Blackburn Rovers and England player, Ronnie Clayton, had taken over from me at Morecambe and I then took over from him!" 1971/72 was the end of Ken's involvement in football and he left the game in May 1972 to work for Reddifusion, and later took up a position with the North West Water Authority. These days Ken and Dorothy live in retirement, in a lovely rural village near Lancaster. He very rarely attends football matches these days, although he is a member of the Preston North End Former Players Association.

Barry Webster

Barry left Rotherham United and signed for Bradford City in June 1962 in exchange for a fee of £7,000. Speaking on 9th June 2005, Barry recalled: "City's manager at the time was Bob Brocklebank, the former Birmingham City manager. I played in most of the games in my first season there but got injured in my second season and never got back my place. After that I played in the Reserves and recall scoring a hat trick away at Workington Reserves. Brian Sawyer joined me at City and we used to go together to training and matches with me driving my first car, an Austin A40."

Barry Webster at his home in the Jordanthorpe area of Sheffield, on 9th June 2005. (Adrian Booth)

Altogether Barry made 53 League appearances for the Bantams and netted nine goals, but City marked the end of his League career and, when released by Bradford City at the end of the 1963/64 season, he drifted into the non-league scene at Buxton. He recalls: "Myself and Brian Sawyer signed for Buxton, whose manager was Norman Curtis, and I played two seasons there. In 1966/67 I played for Thorne Colliery FC along with Peter Perry, after which I spent three seasons as player-manager and two seasons as manager of Norton Woodseats. I finished off my footballing days with three seasons, up to 1974/75, as manager of Smithywood WMC in the Sheffield Sunday League." Outside football, Barry started his own grocery business whilst at Bradford City, and later spent eleven years working for Laycock Engineering. He played nine seasons as an all-rounder with Sykes Cricket Club in the Norton & District League and later enjoyed crown green bowling. Unfortunately, Barry's football legacy has been to suffer with arthritic ankles and consequently he was forced to give up bowling. Looking around for a sport that could accommodate arthritis, he took up fishing, which he enjoys to this day. These days Barry and his wife live in retirement in the Jordanthorpe area of Sheffield, but he retains a keen interest in Rotherham United and is a big fan and supporter of the Nostalgia Society.

Don Weston

Don Weston was transferred to Leeds United in December 1962 and played for them until season 1965/66. He cost Don Revie a fee of £17,000 according to one published source, or £7,500 in another publication. Leeds United's *Official Handbook 1993-94* provides a listing of every player's individual career records, which shows that Weston played 68 League games for Leeds (24 goals) and 10 Cup matches (2 goals). Don was well regarded at Leeds United and nearly played in the F.A. Cup Final when Leeds United played Liverpool at Wembley on 1st May 1965. Although he played in cup-ties leading up to the final, he did not make the Wembley side, although he is shown on page 5 of the cup final programme in a Leeds United team group photograph. Of the fifteen players, Don is sitting extreme left of the front row. When spoken to at his home near Mansfield on 2nd January 2005, Don said: "I was devastated when I did not make the final side, but overall I really enjoyed my time at Leeds United and they had some great players. I was good pals with Jack Charlton and we still keep in touch". In fact the author was shown a recently received Christmas card signed by Jack Charlton and his wife. Don went on to play for Huddersfield Town, whose manager was Tom Johnston who had previously signed him for Rotherham United. A fee of £12,000 secured him from Leeds United on 15th October 1965 and the book *Huddersfield Town – 75 Years On* by George Binns, published by Huddersfield Town FC in 1984, confirms he went on to make twenty League, six substitute League, and one F.A. Cup appearance for Town during seasons 1965/66 and 1966/67, scoring seven League goals. Don then moved in December 1966 back to his first club, Wrexham, where he clocked up a further 42 League games (19 goals). His professional career ended with season 1968/69 as reserve team player-coach at Chester,

Don Weston proudly shows off his runners-up tankard at his home near Mansfield, on 2nd January 2005. (Adrian Booth)

although he did make three League appearances without scoring. Don then drifted into the non-league scene with Altrincham. His total League appearance record was 274 games and 97 goals. Speaking further on 2nd January 2005, Don recalled: "After I packed up football I got a job as a car salesman with the Vauxhall main dealers in Mansfield. Using my contacts at Leeds United, I went back to Elland Road and sold some cars to their Directors! I stayed for fifteen years with the company and became a member of the car manufacturers Guild of Salesmasters." Keith Bambridge recalls a funny incident from that era, saying: "Don called in at a former players Christmas 'do' but nobody recognised him at first as he was wearing an immaculate suit and tie!" Now in retirement, Don has not watched a football match for a long time. He and his wife have lived for many years near their roots in Mansfield, where one of Don's greatest pleasures has been walking out in the countryside with their beloved dogs.